The Reciprocal Translation Project

中美诗人互译计划

The Reciprocal Translation Project
中美诗人互译计划

6 Chinese and 6 US Poets Translate Each Other
中美 12 诗人交互翻译

Editors 主编:
James Sherry 詹姆斯 谢里 *& Sun Dong* 孙冬

Roof Books 屋顶出版社
New York 纽约

ISBN: 978-1-931824-72-9
Library of Congress Control Number: 2017953575

Cover design by Deborah Thomas

Special thanks to our literal translators: Margaret Ross, Feng Chen, Xiao-bo
Yuan, Liuyu Chen & Huang Fan and also to Rebecca Teich

.

NEW YORK | Council on
STATE OF | the Arts   This book is made possible, in part, by the New York State
Council on the Arts with the support of Governor Andrew Cuomo and the
New York State Legislature.

Roof Books
are published by
Segue Foundation
300 Bowery, New York, NY 10012
seguefoundation.com

Roof Books
are distributed by
Small Press Distribution
1341 Seventh Street
Berkeley, CA. 94710-1403
800-869-7553 or spdbooks.org

Table of Contents

Introduction

In *The Reciprocal Translation Project* six Chinese and six American poets have translated each other's works. Since few of these poets speak both languages, bilingual specialists have fashioned literal translations including several options for words that have multiple meanings. These literal translations have been given to three poets in the other language to write poetic translations. In this volume, then, the reader will find an original poem, a literal translation, and three poetic translations of each poem as well as explanatory notes and biographies.

The editors, James Sherry and Sun Dong, propose that the social process of reciprocal translation, engaging several individuals in each translation, has an inherent value. We hope the diverse poems and translations that resulted will help readers in both cultures to apprehend more of the original's intrinsic possibilities—semantic, musical, rhythmic, and prosodic.

In *The Reciprocal Translation Project*, we value spontaneity and difference as much as accuracy and faithfulness. We don't consider deviations from the original meanings as mistakes. Rather we are keen to see how unconventional meanings and language constructions relate to the translator/poet's own culture. We want to represent the complexities involved in the transmission of ideas between cultures.

The reciprocal process also demonstrates greater trust in readers by modifying translation's evaluative hierarchy. Socializing the process of writing, translation, and reading enriches the progression of the works from the world to the author and ultimately to the reader. We'd like our societies to understand each other through difference as well as commonality. Difference of culture and of style helps establish those relationships.

Everybody Likes an Origination Story

In 1991, Zhang Ziqing, editor of the *20th Century History of American Poetry*, and translator, poet, and critic Yunte Huang translated some poems of Hank Lazer, Charles Bernstein, and James Sherry and published the translations under the title *Language Poems*[1]. Lazer and Sherry's book tour in China introduced them to many young writers, most working as part of the group called Original Poets. These poets wrote what they called, perhaps for our benefit, Language Poetry, which for them meant focusing on the Chinese characters with the oldest etymology, often agriculturally based characters. This strategy was quite different from what US poets called Language Writing, which involved procedural strategies, appropriation of various kinds, and linguistic displacement, generating as many different results as there were poets.

Then, in 2014, a young US scholar of Chinese poetry, Margaret Ross, whose parents were friends of Sherry's, showed up in New York having translated one of those Original Poets, Huang Fan, now a nationally important writer and scholar in China. Considering the coincidence as a call to publish, Huang Fan introduced Sherry to Sun Dong and together Sun and Sherry agreed to co-edit a book that became *The Reciprocal Translation Project*. The translation method that Sherry and Sun devised, described above, seemed like a way to bridge the gap between the abstractions of Chinese language that create a specific poetry and specific English vocabulary used to create an abstract poetry.

Translations in Question

Modern poets have collectively evolved many methods to transport poetry between languages. Translators have rewritten the original poem, translated each word literally, transformed the culture of the poem, substituted words based on their sounds (homolinguistic translation), and presented multiple versions of a single poem. Some translations follow the well-thumbed musical idea of theme and variations.

In *19 Ways of Looking at Wang Wei*, Eliot Weinberger supported by Octavio Paz[2] published many translations of the same poem, revealing the limits of any single, definitive translation of Chinese poetry into English. A few years later, Yunte Huang translated a group of classical Chinese poems into English in *Shi*[3], including in the translation a poetic English version, literal translations of both the characters and radicals, what is in each language that doesn't appear in the other, and a series of historical notes, extending the translation of an 8-line poem to four pages—multiplicity in several dimensions.

Sinologist Perry Link in his review of a recent translation of the novel *The Golden Lotus* (金瓶梅 *Jin Ping Mei*) says of three versions of a single paragraph, "None of these translations can be called wrong, or even 'more right' than any other. In each case the translator has grasped the original well, but then, in turning to the needs of second-language readers, handles dilemmas differently."[4] Link, Huang, and Weinberger/Paz all concur that no single translation fully iterates the original. Translation, especially from languages as different as Chinese and English, can only be accomplished within ranges.

In China, the problems of "foreignization" and "domestication" have been discussed in translation studies for decades. The modern Chinese novelist and translator Lu Xun advocated "foreignizing translation." In contrast to American scholar Lawrence Venuti, who proposed the foreignizing strategy to shield the colonized language from the ideological and linguistic intrusion of the colonizer, Lu Xun deferentially used "foreignizing translation" as a means to modernize and enrich the target language (Chinese in this case). Other scholars such as Yan Fu, Lin Shu, Liang Qichao, and Xu Yuanchong prioritized cultural acceptance and aesthetic value over faithfulness to what the translator perceives as the original.

The dichotomies of the different theories of translation has been questioned by scholars such as Zhang Chuanbiao and Gao Jian. They agree that a range of methods are justified if we take into consideration the differences in the purpose of translation, the types of texts, the aesthetic effect, the intention of the author, and the interests of the reader.

The ethics of translation suggest further intrigue along these lines. The Roman chestnut of the translator as traitor (*traduttore, traditore*) raises the question not only of the accuracy of the translation, but also the translation's intent. In recent years, some scholars, such as French sociologist Robert Escarpit, adopted this critique, calling it "Creative Treason" and using it to map the perimeters of a translation practice that takes greater liberties with the original texts to achieve better aesthetic effects in the target language.

Many modern translators present themselves as poets, not simply facilitators of communication. Revaluing translation in this way brings the translator out of the shadow of the author, leveling their identities. In general, English language translators are trending toward the Chinese philosophy of organism that suggests that the poem and the translation act in concert rather than as cause and effect or original and derivative.

Mind the Gap

Exploring links and differences between contemporary Chinese and American poetry is crucial to *The Reciprocal Translation Project*. Many translations subordinate such investigations to emphasize the original poem and its "true" translation to flatter the reader's effort and to exploit commercial possibilities. After all, reading poetry is often difficult. Why put additional obstacles in the reader's path?

But for us, the differences between Chinese and American poetry create opportunities rather than posing threats. In a wonderful conversation with Xi Chuan that we had in a bleach-scented TGI Friday's on Union Square in New York, Xi Chuan pointed out that Chinese and American poets had different ideas of avant garde. For Chinese poets today, avant garde means poetry with political content while in America avant garde implies formal experimentation.

Chinese and American poets also have different expectations about poetry and its role in society. For example, few politicians in America will be exercised about a poem that questions policy, although conservatives attempted to defund the National Endowment for the Arts on religious grounds. In China, on the other hand, the Misty Poets were treated by the political class as a significant protest. Traditional Chinese culture holds that one of the purposes of writing is to convey truth and awaken the awareness of the people. American society politely ignores its poets, expecting them to be entertainers or purveyors of beauty and ideas for a society mired in power politics and debauched violence. How can these two poetic conditions come together?

Looking at Xi Chuan over a cup of fast food coffee that he held, poised above a dilapidated Danish, we agreed that *The Reciprocal Translation Project* made difference a theme to investigate and heterogeneity a value rather than a threat to anyone's literary position, method of translation, or cultural identity. Chinese landscape paintings use this multi-point perspective as a technique that gives the viewer a sense of scale even on a small painting. Difference and its corresponding multiple perspectives remains as much a fact as similarity.

The Reciprocal Translation Project reorients the relationships between poet and translator. Rather than each side presenting their positions for bi-lateral negotiation, *The Reciprocal Translation Project* suggests that we ask the same question of a number of people and then read our path through the alternatives they present. Each translation presents one or more aspects of the original; together they make a multi-dimensional frame that might more closely resemble the vitality and complex possibilities of the original poems.

Translators in Question

Our process in *The Reciprocal Translation Project* avoids exclusivity, but attempts to present poetries that are, taken together, remarkably various. The resulting translations are, themselves, insistently various. As we move away from inaccessible accuracy, what Burton Watson calls "really at last get[ting]

11

the original"[5], difference becomes informative. Chinese words and poems rarely have equivalents in English. As Link says "even grammatical categories are different."[6] While Chinese nouns are often more abstract, the Chinese juxtapositional syntax makes it what Feng Chen, our illustrious literal translator, calls an "exact language".

"Firstly, there are numerous Chinese homonyms; even when the same sound is broken down into four different tones, each sound in a given tone may in reality be a representation of a dozen or even dozens of entirely different words, known in Chinese as characters, with distinct meanings of their own. Secondly, while each Chinese character or word often has single or multiple meanings, in usage it can be and often is combined with another word character to form a word group, with both characters used as the equivalents of word root, prefix or suffix as found in English. The combination fine tunes, changes or significantly alters the meanings of the two characters involved. A change of one word also helps lend shades and nuances to the word group.

"In addition to the contextual and syntactical functions that also contribute to the understanding that Weinberger must have mentioned and possibly exaggerated (as well as the reader's educational background and ability of logical analysis), the above-mentioned two features make Chinese one of the most defined and exact languages as far as I know it (as a language professional). This is particularly true of contemporary Chinese of the past hundred years."[7]

All of our literal translators—Feng Chen, Margaret Ross, Xiao-bo Yuan, Liuyu Chen, Sun Dong, & Huang Fan—looked at the whole process of translation. They worked in a collaborative way, so that no literal translation is the product of one translator.

The Differences Are the Same

Chinese and American poetry both maintain traditions of poets writing within the cultural mainstream and poets writing in solitude. Both have traditions of love poetry, war poetry, personal narrative, religious poetry, nature poetry and epic. Both have traditions of political poetry. In China, politics and literature are an odd couple engaging voluntarily and also involuntarily in ambivalent relationships. Many great Chinese classical poets, Li Po, Du Fu, and Su Shi, for instance, took their art as a way to voice the suffering of their countries and fellow countrymen. The early 20th century political themes of the "New Culture Movement" and the "May Fourth Movement" echoed the Western impetus toward vernacular poetry. New Poetry, as it was called in comparison to classical poetry, was expected to awaken the national awareness of fighting against imperialists and building a modern China.

Later in the Cultural Revolution, poetry suffered a setback as political significance was prioritized at the cost of all other values in literature. In the 1970s, the masked political agenda in Misty poetry served the people's needs to assert individual thinking and free expression while avoiding exposure to danger amid the political turbulence during the recovery years. Gu Cheng, for example, one of the Misty Poets, wrote the poem "Early Spring" to portray the political climate after the downfall of the Extreme Leftists in the early 1980s.

Meanwhile, in the Americas politically active writers from Neruda to Ginsberg wrote with directly political content. Others, such as Language writers, enhanced multiple themes with formal innovations designed to focus on the materiality of language in a way that echoed the Chinese revolutionary political agenda, using prosody politically, rather than overt political themes.

We mean to show that differences are interwoven with similarities. And there are similarities. As Lu Chi (陆机) points out in the classic *Wen Fu* (*The Art of Poetry*, 《文赋》), "Surely, facility with language / and the charging of the word with energy // are effects that can be achieved / by various means."[8] Lu's concept is surely consistent with many Western poetic theories and with little *sturm und drang* differentiates what we call poetry from other writing.

Execution Diverges

The poets we have chosen for *The Reciprocal Translation Project* are some of their nations' leading writers. Detailed biographies are at the end of the book. Rae Armantrout, Mei-mei Berssenbrugge, Huang Fan, Lan Lan, Fred Moten, Na Ye, Bob Perelman, Wang Xiaoni, and Xi Chuan are all widely translated international figures. Che Qianzi, Brandon Brown, and Nada Gordon are young, innovative writers working with formal invention. Two of the women poets we selected—Wang Xiaoni and Na Ye—are of minority ethnic groups (Manchu nationality). Among the Americans we have multiple races and ethnic groups. In fact, all the poets are well known but different from each other, so that *The Reciprocal Translation Project* presents a variety of innovative styles, linguistic strategies, and biographies.

The US poets involved in this process are mostly postmodernists. They are interested in psychological and political nuances, racial identities, cross border explorations, and playful experiments with words that explore political issues. Among the Chinese poets, Che Qianzi, Xi Chuan, and Wang Xiaoni lean more toward postmodernism than do the modernists, Huang Fan, Lan Lan, and Na Ye.

The Chinese poets in the *Reciprocal Translation Project*, for the most part, are more concerned with the crises in social life, history, and being an individual in history. For many Chinese poets, language experiments are secondary considerations with Che Qianzi, another of the Original Poets, being the exception. Language experiments are sometimes considered as frivolous and an obstruction to the presentation of reality be it social or psychological.

There are similarities and differences in the ways the poets finally translated the other language. We would have to write another book to describe all the tactics and strategies these 12 poets used. Some of the poets, like Lan Lan, Huang Fan, Na Ye, Mei-mei Berssenbrugge, and Xi Chuan translate to capture the essence of the poem without deviating too much from the literal, making their prosody more energetic and convincing than the literal

14

translation. In their translations, they try to negotiate with the postmodern aesthetics by bridging the inconsistencies and combing through the labyrinth of sometimes convoluted syntactic structures. Xi Chuan, the Chinese poet most fluent in English, seems intent on capturing the original meaning and rhythms of English language.

Some poets like Nada Gordon and Che Qianzi transform the poem into the other culture, bringing a new dimension of associations and significance. Some poets like Brandon Brown write their translations as a kind of commentary on how poetry gets written and how this specific instance appears. Che Qianzi wrote a poem entitled "Lizard—to Dong Sun, Group Photo: A Reconstruction of Fred Moten, Bob Perelman, Mei-mei Berssenbrugge's Poems" to comment on their poems as well as the translation process. Lan Lan and Wang Xiaoni create a hybrid poem/prose lineation from Brandon Brown's prose block in "Catullus 108". Slight variations in one translation explode into open insurrection in the next translation. The surfaces remain tempestuous throughout.

While some poets attempt to bridge the gaps and the inconsistencies of intention, others are trying to disrupt the textual structures and syntactic coherences. Other things that these poets' translations do is change the mode of address, change the timing, add or subtract a layer of reference, invoke a new place or priority. As we have said, these possibilities are also multiple.

These translations also highlight how our view of poetry changes as we change roles from poet to translator and back. As poets, we consider our own personal criteria, where we diverge from received language, and the issues of the day. As translators, we write, interpret, and rewrite poetry. As editors, we also consider the purpose, strategies, and tactics of the poets to determine whether they have fulfilled their intention in a useful, new, or elegant way. As publishers, we consider readership as well as timing and the relationship between poets and different kinds of readers. As readers, when we read outside those professional roles, letting the writer guide us, raise questions when we disagree or have difficulty understanding, and compare them to how it matches our experience with this language, this theme, this form, and this poem.

Having a broader set of criteria available for translation also allows poetry to adapt to changing conditions in the societies surrounding it. Here's an approach to international poetry that gives poetry and poetics a seat at the table when discussing how to mediate diverse cultures.

James Sherry 詹姆斯 谢里 *& Sun Dong* 孙冬

1. Szechuan Press, 1991.
2. New York: Moyer Bell, 1987 & New Directions, 2016.
3. New York: Roof, 1997.
4. "A Wonderfully Elusive Chinese Novel", *New York Review of Books*, April 23, 2015.
5. *Chinese Rhyme-Prose* (New York-Hong Kong: The Chinese University of Honk Kong Press-New York Review of Books, 1971-2015). Sam Hamill translator.
6. Link, Op. Cit.
7. Email from Feng Chen to James Sherry 08/16/2015.
8. Lu Chi, *Wen Fu* (Minneapolis: Milk Weed Editions, 2000), trans. Sam Hamill.

雷伊 艾尔曼特罗特 / Rae Armantrout

原诗 Original Poem

View

Not the city lights. We want

-the moon-

                      The Moon
None of our own doing!

直译 Literal Translation

视觉

不是城市的灯光。我们想要

·——月亮——·

                      月亮非我们
所为

诗译 Poetic Translations

目击

我们想要的——月亮——
不是城市的灯光可以攀比

                      月亮
不是我们造的，又与我们有关

—translated by Huang Fan 黄梵译

视觉

不是城市的灯光。我们想要

月亮

月亮我们不能制造

—translated by Na Ye 娜夜译

视觉

不要说城市的灯光。我们想要

——月亮——

月亮

那和我们完全没关系的弱光

—translated by Wang Xiaoni 王小妮译

原诗 Original Poem

Arrivals

Sign in the airport:
It's not how much
Cloud,
but what kind.

*

Welcome.
"We don't play requests,
but we don't play bagpipes
either. We figure
that's fair."

That's the bad-boy
sass
of globalization

kick-starting you
on Clear Channel

where even the spin
gets spun.

    *

Here's one:

The devil is a blowsy,
failed executive

who fires burn-outs,
star after star.

    *

Every known object
rotates

as if:

    b. keeping busy
    c. stunned

直译 Literal Translation

抵达

机场里的标牌/广告：
重要的不在于多大
云 [1]，
而是什么样的云。

     *

欢迎。
"我们不玩点播，但我们也不播放风笛 [2]。
我们觉得/想
这样（做）是公平的。

那是坏男孩 无礼/粗鲁的
全球化

在"清晰频道信息公司"
将你开动/助你创业 [3]

那里，甚至那些忽悠人的
也被忽悠 [4]。

     *

跟你讲个笑话/故事/告诉你吧

魔鬼是邋遢的

失败/失意的管理人员/经理 [5]

他把身心疲惫的人/没用的人 解雇。

一个星星接着一个星星 [6]

*

每一个已知物体
都在旋转

似乎：

    b. 不停地繁忙/停不下来 [7]
    c. 惊愕

译注 Notes & Explanations

1. 可以指代云彩以及数字云。
2. 指难听的音乐。
3. 为首次创业提供资金。原义为用脚踩动来发动摩托车。
4. 指的是政治公关、制造舆论等。
5. 诗人本人讲这个意象是受到了特朗普的电视讲话和他竞选总统的事实的启发。
6. 星星指代那些曾经为公司贡献生命、曾经熠熠生辉的人。
7. 注意，字母"b"和"c"之前跳过了字母 "a"。

诗译 Poetic Translations

抵达

机场广告：
不在于云
有多大，
而在于是什么样的云。

*

欢迎
不玩点播，
也不播放风笛录音。
我们觉得
这样最公平。

那坏男孩已有着
全球化的无礼

高清频道
将帮助你创业

谁忽悠人
谁也会被人忽悠

　　　　*

跟你讲个笑话
告诉你吧，魔鬼总是邋遢的
是失败的公司经理
他要解雇身心疲惫的人
那一颗又一颗璀璨之星

你已知的每个东西
都像星星一样旋转

似乎

　　b）停不下来
　　c）惊愕不已

—translated by Huang Fan 黄梵译

抵达

机场里的指示牌：并不需要很大
云什么样子很重要。

　欢迎

"我们不玩点播，但我们也不吹风笛。
这很公平。
那是坏男孩
有着全球化的莽撞

在"清晰频道信息公司"你得到了启示
旋转者也被旋转
告诉你吧魔鬼是邋遢的
失意的总裁
他把身心疲惫的人解雇。
星星挨着星星

似乎：
每一个事物
都在旋转
—translated by Na Ye 娜夜译

抵达

机场的广告牌
多大一块不重要
云
重要的是云的样子

欢迎。

"我们不玩点播
不过 也不放差的音乐
我们觉得这样才公平
坏男孩的粗鲁的全球化
在"清晰信息公司"
帮你启动了
那里连忽悠人的人也被忽悠了

给你说一个笑话
魔鬼邋遢
失败的管理者
他把累到极限的人给辞退
一个又一个曾经额头灵光闪烁的人

所有已知的物体都在运转

……

    B，不累吗
    C，不得了了

—*translated by Wang Xiaoni 王小妮译*

原诗 Original Poem

SOFT MONEY

They're sexy
because they're needy,
which degrades them.

They're sexy
because they don't need you.

They're sexy because they pretend
not to need you,

but they're lying,
which degrades them.

They're beneath you
and it's hot.

They're across the border,
rhymes with dancer—

they don't need
to understand.

They're content to be
(not *mean*),

which degrades them
and is sweet.

They want to be
the thing-in-itself

and the thing-for-you—

Miss Thing—

but can't.

They want to be you,
but can't,

which is so hot.

直译 Literal Translation

软钱 [1]

它们/她们/他们很性感
因为它们/她们/他们有需要/粘人,
这贬低了它们/她们/他们。

它们/她们/他们性感,因为
他们/她们/它们不需要你。

它们/她们/他们有性感,因为它们/她们/他们假装
不需要你。

但它们/她们/他们在说谎,
这贬低了它们/她们/他们

它们/她们/他们低于你/在你身下
而且骚热。

它们/她们/他们跨越疆界而来
与舞者同韵—

它们/她们/他们不需要 [2]
去理解。
它们/她们/他们满足于存在
并不在乎是否有意义

这贬低了它们/她们/他们
而且是甜蜜的/贴心的

它们/她们/他们想要成为
物自身

以及给为你—之—物—³

东西小姐——

但办不到。

它们/她们/他们想成为你，
但办不到，

这真是性感风骚。

译注 Notes & Explanations

1. 软性政治捐献, 以规避联邦规定或限制的方法做出的政治捐献
2. 诗人自己解释说这是从杜兰杜兰（Duran Duran）乐团的《里约》这
    首歌的部分歌词改写而来。原歌词大概是这样的：她的名字叫里
    约。她不需要理解。啊，里约，里约舞者，跨过大里约河。杜兰杜
    兰乐队是 1980 年代至今历久不衰的英美流行音乐乐团之一，开创了
    所谓"华丽摇滚"、"新浪漫主义"之乐风。他们的乐风以"新
    潮"为主旋律，过去 30 年里他们有 21 首单曲荣膺"美国流行音乐
    排行榜前 100 名"，缔造售出 8500 万张唱片的辉煌纪录。
3. "物自身"和"为我之物"是康德哲学中的概念。

诗译 Poetic Translations

软钱

它们、她们、他们都很性感
如果因为需要
这就贬低了它们、她们、他们。

它们、她们、他们性感，只因为
他们、她们、它们已不需要你。

它们、她们、他们有点性感，因为它们、她们、他们假装
已不需要你。

如果它们、她们、他们说谎，
这就真贬低了它们、她们、他们

它们、她们、他们如果跪下来，在你身下
风骚。

它们、她们、他们将会越界
与舞者同谋——

它们、她们、他们已不需要
理解。
它们、她们、他们满足于活着
并不在乎意义

这当然贬低了它们、她们、他们
是甜蜜的贬低

它们、她们、他们就想成为
物

以及侍候我的物

比如，称呼为东西小姐——

这办不到啊。

比如，它们、她们、他们都想成为你，
但办不到啊。

这才真正性感、风骚。

—*translated by Huang Fan 黄梵译*

软钱

她们性感 她们被需要，这使她们卑贱。

她们性感，因为她们不需要你。

她们性感，因为她们假装
不需要你。

她们说谎，
她们卑贱

她们在你身体之下
风情万种。

她们毫无禁忌
舞蹈般扭动着肉体

她们不需要理解。
她们满足于此并不在乎意义

她们卑贱而快乐

她们想让性成为
性本身

成为　　为你所用的
东西小姐——

但办不到。

她们想成为你，
也办不到，

这更加撩拨人心

—translated by Na Ye 娜夜译

软钱

所有的他们都性感
因为所有的他们都有这需求
所有的他们被轻蔑了

他们性感 因为他们
对你没有需求

他们性感 因为他们装作
不需要你
但他们在说谎
这是轻蔑了他们

他们在你的身体下面
骚动滚烫

他们从远处一跃而来
加入了舞者的节奏

他们不需要

去理解
他们在这世界上很满足
对意义完全不在乎

这轻蔑了他们
而且是甜蜜的
他们想要成为物自身

还有为—我—之—物

小姐

但不行

他们想成为你
但是不行

真是热啊。

—translated by Wang Xiaoni 王小妮译

白萱华 / **Mei-mei Berssenbrugge**

原诗 Original Poem

WINTER WHITES

1

Now memory widens its focus.

An experience is not one experience.

I go over it again and again, as it assimilates in me.

Repeating becomes more like an associative process.

I can't depend on an event so thinking of it, it's instantly categorized, as if by a student.

I follow as it slips beyond the border of my recall, where repeating becomes progressive.

And memory doesn't end where my skin ends, but diffuses into my surroundings, leaving fragments of itself I may notice as "red rock," "friable cliff," reminding me.

2

Looking into sky and so backward in time depends on my belief in origins and on the effects of my attention.

There, a butterfly is a live portion of earth flying, deer a portion of its leafy surface.

Forgetting loses indeterminance as it fills out the plane of immanence, like the universe in infinity.

34

My so-called memory of my experience is an index, in which self comes into being at the same time as the butterfly.

That's why environment can't be identified by a consciousness that's coextensive with it.

More and more an experience becomes a contingent particle.

Recognizing and observing combine into a relation or inference fueled by emotion as by low tones of his voice, a limit or association based on partiality—my interest, my mother, family, certain writers, western light—as when I look at his image in a magazine, I think of Richard who isn't here.

Then I look for the invisible wires of this passage.

3

Between any experiences, memories, objects are silent rhythms and intervals.

I go over an event as it develops beyond anxiety at whether a blank is in my mind and red rock in the world or whether transparency *is* landscape.

Sunlight, night, despair and gems or solitude, reef, star dissolving into names make eventless the poet's experience.

Your face before me is an epiphany for distance and crossing.

It's not a dialectic of self-other, like threads of pink light through mist *or* pink veins of a petal on my desk.

Mist and petal together form their own pathway, percepts threading back and forth as if through live wires in air.

Hue accumulates around my intense desire to recall.

My mood changes with slices of color into reality I categorize as afternoon sky; pink disintegrating in the petal is a transparent vein.

Its form represents materialized accumulated energies moving toward me, when I tried to express the amnesia, immanence leading me from a photograph to recast light onto experience, until identification, sameness became the atmosphere.

4

A white out of wintry weather: I did not think feeling proceeded from anything *like* this.

Details of landscape is how a person losing her memory visualizes the panoply of experience.

Recalling a face is only part of the visual; there's turbulence between light reflecting from your face into my brain and my emotion as one-to-one recollection from an ideal vantage point.

Light itself is forming darkness and spectrums exist outside light's laws.

Spaces in my living room between objects or spaces between stars are only symbols; blankness is filled with experience.

A collective unconscious of all experience underlies events along an electron's path, because space is a psychological property.

I don't pinpoint your location like a chair and bureau on a dreamed floor.

I see light around a corner, combinations of others' memories adjacent to mine and polyvalent.

Instead of blankness, fear takes the form of an argument in the family or a series of frightful dreams.

An event can weave through these manifestations, dissipating itself along with my own borders.

Illness turns into such a nightmare, but self maintains, operating as a wave.

Different species communicate and energies of environment and inhabitants merge.

My memory travels into the memory of another with increasing energy, and an event clarifies as "winter," for example.

直译 Literal Translation

冬天的白色/空白

1

现在记忆放大/拓宽它的焦点。

一个/一次经验不是/一次一个经验。

我一次次地重温（这个经验），它也在被我吸收、同化。

重复变得更像是一个联想/联系的过程。

我无法依靠/信任对于一个事件的印象/看法，一旦想到它，它旋即被归类，似乎是一个学生所为。

我跟随着它，越过我记忆的藩篱/边界，那里，重复成为进行中的/前进的。

在我的肌肤/身体终止之处，记忆并没有终止，而是蔓延到我周遭一切，留自我的碎片——在我看来可能是"红色的岩石"和"松脆的悬崖"，提醒着我。

2

望向天空，时间向后退去，后退致何处，有赖于我对起源的信仰以及我关注的成效。

那里，一只蝴蝶是飞行中的大地的活生生的一部分，鹿是它落满树叶的表面的一块 。

忘却丧失了模糊/不确定性，当它填满了急迫的平面，像无限的宇宙。

我对于经验的所谓的记忆是一个指数，其间自我与蝴蝶同时萌生。

那就是为什么环境不能由和其相生的意识界定/不能等同于和它相生的意识。

经验越来越多地成为一个偶然的粒子/颗粒。

受情感激发，像被他低沉的声调感染， 认识和观察结合成一种关系或者推论，一种基于偏面认识/酷爱/偏爱的局限或者联想—我的兴趣，我的母亲，家庭，某些作家，西方的光——当我在一本杂志上看到他的形象，我想到不在场的理查。

然后我寻找这段文字无形的线 。

3
在任何经验，记忆和物体之间贯穿沉默的节奏和间隔。

我回顾一个事件，当它继续发展，超越了这样的焦虑/不再焦虑地思考：空白是否在我的头脑中，红色岩石是否在世界上，或者透明是否是[1]一种景色。

阳光，夜晚，绝望以及宝石和孤独，暗礁，星星溶解成为名字，使得诗人的经验平淡无奇。

你的脸在我面前是对于距离和跨越的顿悟。

它不是自我和他者的辩证法，像透过薄雾的粉色光束或者我书桌上一个花瓣的粉色脉络。

薄雾和花瓣一起构成他们自己的路径，印象/感觉前后穿行似乎穿过空中的电线。

在我强烈的回忆的欲望四周，色彩在累积。

我的情绪起伏变化，随着片片颜色进入我命名为下午天空的现实之中；花瓣里的分解的粉色是透明的脉络。
它的形态是累积着的力量的物质再现，它向我奔来，当我试图表达失忆症，迫切的环境促使我/引领我走出一张照片，对于一个经验投射新的视角，直到同化变成了/统一了周围的环境/氛围。

4

从寒冬的季节/天气里散发的一缕白色：我从未想到感觉竟然从这里滋生。

景色的细致之处是/在于一个人如何丧失了她记忆中经验之林林总总的画面。

回忆一张脸只是图像的一部分，将你的脸反射进入我的头脑的光线和我从一个最佳角度进行的一对一追溯的情感之间发生了一些动荡/骚乱。光本身正在产生光的法则之外的黑暗和谱系。

在我的客厅物件之间的空间以及星星之间的距离都只不过是象征；经验填满了空白。

事件之下，所有经验的集体无意识，沿着电子的路径而行，因为空间是一种心理的属性在梦中的地上，我不会锁定你的位置，像对椅子和书桌一样。

我看见不远处的光，（他们是）和我的记忆接壤的他人记忆的集合，众多分子的合体[2]。恐惧在家庭里或者一系列可怕的梦境中呈现为一种观点，而不是（完全的）空白。

一个事件可以在这些显像里编织，和我的边界一道慢慢消散。

疾病变成这样一个噩梦，但自我保留着，像波浪一样运动/运行。

不同的物种交流，环境的能量和栖居者合而一体。

我的记忆游荡，进入另一人的记忆，带着渐强的能量，一个事件被澄清为/宣布为"冬天"，比如。

译注 Notes & Explanations
1. 原文的"is"是斜体。

2. 多价体是一个细胞遗传学的概念。在多倍体减数分裂中的第一次成熟分裂前期的偶线期中同源染色体联会 (synapsis)，联会的结果使同源染色体形成一个多价体，此时，每条染色体由两条姊妹染色单体组成。

诗译 Poetic Translations

空白

1.
现在记忆冲扩它的焦点。

一个经验不是一次。

我一次次重温，它被我加热、融化。

重复变得像联想工程。

我无法信任对于一个事件的看法，想到它，旋即归类，像学生功课。

我跟随它，越过记忆边界，那里，重复成为进步。

在我身体终止之处，记忆没有终止，弥漫周遭，自我的碎片——在我看来可能是"红岩"和"松崖"，提醒着我。

2.
望向天空，时间后退，后退到哪一步，有赖于我对起源的信仰以及我关注的成效。

那里，一只蝴蝶是飞行中的大地活生生的一部分，鹿是它落满树叶的表面一块。

忘却丧失模糊，当它填满急迫的平面，像宇宙无限。

我对于经验的记忆是个指数，其间，自我与蝴蝶同时剥茧。

为什么环境不能等同于和它相生的意识。

经验越来越多成为偶然粒子。

受情感激发，像被他低沉的声调感染，认识和观察结合成推理，基于偏面，酷爱的局限——我的兴趣，我的母亲，家庭，某些作家，西方的光——当我在一本杂志上看到他的形象，我想到不在场的理查。

然后我寻找这段文字无形的线。

3.
在经验、记忆和物体之间贯穿沉默的节奏和间隔。

我回顾一个事件，当它继续发展，超越这样的焦虑：空白是否在头脑，红岩是否在世界，或者透明是否一种景色。

阳光，夜晚，绝望以及宝石和孤独，暗礁，星星溶解成为名字，使得诗人的经验平淡无奇。

你的脸在我面前是对于距离和跨越的顿悟。

它不是自我和他者的辩证法，像透过薄雾的粉色光束或者我书桌上一个花瓣的粉色脉络。薄雾和花瓣一起构成他们自己的路径，印象前后步行似乎穿过空中的电线。

我强烈的回忆，这欲望四周，色彩在加浓。

我的情绪起伏变化，随着片片颜色进入我命名为下午天空的现实之中；花瓣里分解的粉色是透明的脉络。

它的形态累积着物力再现，它向我奔来，当我试图表达失忆症，迫切的环境引领我走出一张照片，对于一个经验投射新的视角，直到融化变成氛围。

4

从寒冬的天气里散发一缕白色：我从未想到感觉竟然在这里滋生。

景色细致之处在于一个人如何丧失她记忆中经验的林林总总画面。

回忆一张脸只是图像的一部分，将你的脸反射进我头脑的光线和我从最佳角度进行一对一追溯的情感之间发生了动荡。

光本身正在产生光的法则之外的黑暗和谱系。

在我客厅物件之间的空间以及星星之间的距离都只不过是象征；经验填满空白。

事件之下，所有经验的集体无意识，沿着电路而行，因为空间是一种心理属性。

在梦中的地上，我不会定型你的位置，像对椅子和书桌一样。

我看见不远处的光，（他们是）和我记忆接壤的他人记忆的积聚，众多分子的合影。

恐惧在家庭里或者一系列可怕的梦境中呈现为一种观点，而不是（完全的）空白。

一个事件在这些显像里编织，和我的边界一道慢慢消散。

疾病变成这样一个噩梦，但自我保留着，像波浪一样飘荡。

不同的物种交流，环境和栖居者合为一体。

我的记忆游荡，进入另一人的记忆，带着渐强的能量，一个事件被澄清为"冬天"，比如。

—*translated by Che Qianzi 车前子译*

冬之空白

1
现在记忆放大它的焦点。一种经验不是一次经验。

我一次次重历，它亦被我改变。

重历更像建立彼此联系的过程。

我无法信任对于一个事物的印象，一旦想到它，瞬间它就被归类，似乎是一个
忠实的好学生。

我跟随它，越过记忆的樊篱，那里，重复正匍匐前行。

在我肉体结束之处，记忆并没有终止，它蔓延至我周围的一切，留下自我的碎片————
那是"红色岩石"和"脆弱的悬崖"，在提醒我。

2
目光投入长天，时间向后退去。后退到何处，有赖于我如何关注信仰的起源。在那里，一只蝴蝶是飞行中的大地活生生的一部分，鹿是落满它外衣的树叶之其中一枚。

遗忘丧失了不确定性，当它填平急切的路面，就像宇宙在无限里。

对于经验所谓的记忆我只是一个指数，我和蝴蝶在其中同时诞生。

这就是为什么环境不能由和其相生的意识所界定。

经验越来越多地成为一个偶然的粒子。

受感情激发，如同被他低沉的声调感染，认识和观察结合成一种关系或者推论，一种基于片面认识的局限或联想——我的兴趣，我的母亲，家庭，某些作家，西方的
光芒——当我在一本杂志上看到他的形象，我想到不在场的查理。

如此，我开始寻找这段文字无形的线索。

3
在一切经验、记忆和事物之间贯穿沉默的节奏和间隔。

我回想一件事情，但它继续发展，超越了这样的焦虑：空白是否在我的头脑中，红色岩石是否在世界上，或者透明是否"是"一种景色。

阳光，夜晚，绝望以及宝石和孤独，暗礁，星星溶解成为名字，使得诗人的经验平淡无奇。
你的脸在我面前是对距离和跨越的顿悟。

她不是自我和他者的辩证法，想透过薄雾的粉红光束，或者是我书桌上一枚花瓣的粉红脉络。
薄雾和花瓣一起构成它们自己的路径，感觉往复穿行似乎穿越空中的电线。

在我强烈的回忆的欲望四周，色彩在堆积。我的情绪起伏变化，随着斑斑色彩进入我命名为午后天空的现实之中；花瓣分解的粉红是透明的脉络。

它的形态是积累着力量的物质再现，它向我奔来，当我试图表达失忆症，逼仄的环境引导我走出照片，对于一个经验投射新的视角，直到我融化于周遭的一切。

4

寒天拖一缕云烟：我从未想过感觉竟然从中升起。
景色的细节在于一个人如何丧失了记忆中经验繁复的画面。

一张脸在记忆中只是图像的一部分，将你的脸反射进我大脑的光线，以及从最佳角度进行一对一
追忆的情感，这两者之间发生着一场动乱。

光本身正在产生光的法则之外的黑暗和谱系。

在我客厅家具之间的空间以及星星之间的距离只是象征，唯有经验才能填满空白。

事件之下，一切经验的集体无意识，沿电子的路径前行，因为空间是一种心理属性。

在梦中的地板上，我不会锁定你的位置，如同对椅子和桌子那般。

我看见不远处的光，那是和我的记忆接壤的他人记忆的集合，众多分子的多价体融合。

恐惧在家庭里或一系列可怕的梦境呈现为一种观点，并不是完全的空白。

一个事件可以在这些显影剂中成形，和我的边界一道慢慢消融。疾病变成一个噩梦，但自我总会保留，像波浪一样起伏运动。

不同的物种交流，环境的能量和栖居者合为一体。

我的记忆游荡，进入另一个人的记忆，带着逐渐加强的能量，一个事件被宣示为"冬天"，以此为例。

—translated by Lan Lan 蓝蓝译

冬日白色

1
现在记忆扩张它的焦点。

一次经验不是一个经验。

我将它一次次重温，而它也在消化我，在我体内。

重温变得更像一个联结过程。

思索中的事靠不住，它被瞬间归类，这是学生的做法。

而我跟着它，越过我记忆的边界，我的重温在此继续展开。
记忆并不停在我皮肤的表层，它蔓延到我周遭，碎成在我看来可能是
"红岩"和"松脆悬崖"的碎块，提醒着我。

2
我对起源的信仰和凝神的效力决定了我眺望天空，回思往日。

那里，一只蝴蝶是飞翔大地活跃的一部分，鹿是覆满落叶的地表的一部
分。

无限的宇宙，是忘却弥平了万物的沟沟坎坎，失却其不确定性。我对自
我经验的所谓记忆是一个索引，自我生成其中恰当蝴蝶于其中生成。

因此与之共生的意识不能识别环境。

一个经验日渐变成一个随机的粒子。

受情感激发，像被他低沉的声调所感染，认知和观察结合成一种关系或
推论，一种基于偏爱的局限或联想——我的兴趣、我的母亲、家庭、某
些作家、西方的光——当我在一本杂志上看到他的形象，我想到不在场
的理查。

然后我寻找这段文字中看不见的导线。

3
在任何经验、记忆和任何物体之间，都有沉静的节奏和间歇。

我回顾某事，当它继续发展到超越于这样的焦虑：即我头脑中是否有个空白、世上是否有块红色岩石，或透明是不是一片风景。

阳光、夜晚、绝望以及宝物或孤独、暗礁、星星，溶解成名号，令诗人的经验平淡无奇。

你的脸呈现在我面前是距离和跨越的显现。

这不是自我和他者的辩证法，像透过雾气的粉色光束或我桌上一枚花瓣的粉色脉络。

雾气和花瓣共建它们自己的路径，感觉前后穿行仿佛穿过空中的电线。

围绕着我强烈的回忆之欲望，色彩积聚。

我色彩片片的情绪起伏，化为我认作午后天空的现实；花瓣里的粉色分解，乃有透明的脉络。其形态体现着物质化的积聚的能量向我奔来，当我努力表达失忆，固有的一切引领着我从一张照片开始，重新布光，照向经验，直到确认、同一性变得理所当然。

4
冬日的白色一道：我从未想过感觉会从这里滋生。

风景的细节是：丧失记忆的一个人如何使经验的盔甲视觉化。

回忆一张脸只是视觉的一部分；照进我大脑的你脸上的反光、还有从最佳角度一对一回溯的我的情感——在这两者之间有一些波荡。

光本身正在形成存在于光之法则以外的黑暗和光谱。

我客厅内物体之间的空间以及星体之间的空间均不过是象征而已；经验填满了空白。

所有经验的集体无意识沿电子路径铺垫于事件之下，因为空间是一种心理财富。

在梦的地面，我不会锁定你的位置，像对椅子和书桌那样。

我看见不远处的光，那是他人的记忆集合了与之接壤的我的记忆和多价染色体。

恐惧不是空白，它以家庭争执或一系列可怕的梦境为形态。

事件可以编织于显像，与我的边界一道消散。

疾病化作这样的噩梦，但保留下自我，运动如波浪。

不同的物种沟通，环境的能量与栖居者合为一体。

我的记忆游荡入另一个人的记忆，带着渐强的能量，一个事件被澄清为"冬天"，比如说。

—*translated by Xi Chuan 西川译*

布兰登 布朗 / **Brandon Brown**

原诗 Original Poem

PIGS

I would never hold hands with a pig.
But as a vitamin-deprived crackerlet,
my rearers were obsessed with a symbolic play
in which the little stubs hanging off my palms
were pigs. Doing typical pig shit too.
Going to the market. Gumming roast beef.
Slurping trash out of a trough like it was lamb
kidneys in shallot sauce. Sure, I season
my own shapeless chemical dinners with a
little pork product. Inhaling sodium ennui glutamate.
Listening to the lachrymose squeals of an angered
Kardashian, *luving* its peal across the bereft
orchard of my machinery. And I am going to
call a pig a fucking pig. This blonde Franz-type
stalks the halls of my office building.
He nods up with his whole cleft so I can see
the breezy blonde hairs inside his snout shake.
Sparkling honky eyes. He licks his lips
spying spine. Hot lard for a cold
baton. Wild boars still roam the woods
of Marin, but in the streets of Oakland
all you can see are pigs. Saying something sort of
shitty to a garbage collector. I got a ticket for effusive
dumping and the pig thanked me, handing over
carbon copy. Smudging my enduring
dermal affability. I grabbed his tail and pulled
it Botox taut. That's not
compost staining the wrinkles in my fingers, pig.
It's what degrades this beautiful salt-lick

I put clothes on every day: white but pig-hating,
full of lovable rancor. It smells a little yesterday.
Backdated fish. Big potato. What goes
in the garbage. Cognac for pigs.

直译 Literal Translation

猪

我决不会跟猪携手。
但是，对我这个维生素贫乏的小乡巴佬，
我的养育者痴迷于一种象征游戏 [1]
游戏里我的小短枝 [2] 从手掌上悬挂下来是猪。还做着典型的猪屎勾当
前往市场。嚼着烤牛肉。
从槽里边喷喷吃边扒拉出垃圾，仿佛就是
红葱酱里的羊腰子。当然，作为调料，我给我自己
无形/没有形状的化学物晚餐放上了
一点猪肉产品。吸入谷氨无聊酸钠/味无聊精聆
听着一个愤怒的卡戴珊 [3] 悲哀的/眼泪汪汪 [4] 的尖叫
喜欢/稀饭 [5] 它的巨声鸣响响彻我失却的/悲痛的
机器果园。而我要叫一只猪一只
操蛋猪。这个金发的弗朗茨品种 [6]
潜进我办公大楼的各个大厅。
他抬起头来张开整个裂腭，使我能看见
他那摇动猪鼻子里被微风轻抚的金黄毛。
发光的白鬼子眼睛。他舔了舔嘴唇，
用眼睛瞄着那些脊梁。热猪油给冷的警棒。野猪
仍然漫游在马林
树林，但在奥克兰的街头
所有你能看到的都是猪。对收垃圾的人说着有些
难听的/令人厌恶的话。我得到一张罚单，
是因为大量/过量/滔滔不绝的倾倒。那头猪感谢我，（用手）递来

复写页。玷污了我持久的

皮肤的亲和力。我抓住他的尾巴，把它拉得

像（用了）保妥适/肉毒素/肉毒杆菌素/瘦脸针[7]一样绷紧。那不是

堆肥玷污了我手指的皱纹，猪。

就是它降低/贬低了这个美丽的, 盐渍地/盐块[8]

我每天穿上衣服：白色[9]但憎恶猪的，充满着可爱的深仇/怨恨。

闻起来有点昨天（的味道）。

回溯/倒填日期的鱼。大土豆。扔进

垃圾里的东西。干邑给猪喝。

注释 Notes & Explanations

1. 指的是一首英美国家流行的手指儿歌《小小猪》。玩的时候游戏者一边板着五个指头并一边说："一只小猪去市场，一只小猪留在家。一只小猪烤牛肉，一只小猪啥没有。一只小猪呵呵呵，一路乐回家。"下文中的去市场和吃烤牛肉都是游戏的内容。

2. 这里指的是手指头。

3. 金·卡戴珊（Kimberly Noel "Kim" Kardashian) 是一位美国娱乐界名媛、模特和商人。卡戴珊是一种美国流行文化的符号，一种粗俗、浮夸的且无需任何成本和基础的现代流行文化。

4. 这里的 "lachrymose" 有矫情的感伤的意思。

5. Luv，俗语，是喜爱的意思，比 love 随意，这种轻松的用法避免了 love 这个字所包含的沉重的内容。原诗中 luv 使用的是斜体，表示强调。

6. 指代德国人，是美国人对于德国人的略带贬义的叫法。

7. Botox: 保妥适，主要成分为高度纯化的肉毒杆菌素 a 型，是一种神经传导的阻断剂，用以治疗过度活跃的肌肉。作为整形美容材料，主要用于除皱与瘦脸。也是是一种天然、纯化的蛋白质，可让造成皱纹的肌肉放松，肌肤变得平滑、年轻、而且更富有青春活力只要将极少剂量的 保妥适 精确地注射入特定的脸部肌肉，可使动态性的皱纹消失。

8. 供给动物盐和其他矿物质的地方，可以是天然的盐泽地，也可以是人们放在那里的盐块。

9. 可以指衣服的颜色，也可以指皮肤的颜色。

诗译 Poetic Translations

猪

我绝不会跟一头猪合作
但我是个乡巴佬，一个缺维生素的家伙
养我的人喜欢玩象征
玩我手掌悬下来的那些小短枝
这当然是猪。最典型的造猪屎的勾当
是去市场，嚼着烤牛肉。
边吃边从槽里扒出垃圾，
犹如扒出红葱酱里的羊腰子。当然，我把猪肉
当作调料，放进我吃的一顿
化学晚餐。摄入的味精
聆听着眼泪的尖叫
它喜欢稀饭的巨大吸溜声
响彻我早已失去的机械果园，而我想让一头操蛋猪
金发的弗朗茨
潜进我办公楼的各个大厅
它抬头时张开了裂颚，让我看见了
猪鼻子里被风撼动的金毛。
发光的白鬼子的眼睛
它舔着嘴唇，眼睛瞄着脊背。热猪油泼向
冷的警棍。野猪也在马林的树林漫步，而奥克兰的街头
所有的漫步者都是猪。我朝一个拾荒者
吐脏话，得到一张罚单。因为吐得太多
那头猪倒感谢我。递上
复写纸，弄脏了我可爱的
皮肤。我拉住它的尾巴，拉得
比肉毒杆菌还要紧绷。猪，不用
朝我手指的皱纹上施肥啦。
也不要贬低这块美丽的盐渍地
我每天穿衣服：穿上白肤的

可爱的深仇大恨。闻起来又永远是昨天的味道。
鱼也可以找到一个日子，和大土豆一起
被扔进垃圾，风干了再给猪吃。

—translated by Huang Fan 黄梵译

猪

我决不会和一只猪携手。
但是，对我这个维生素贫乏的小乡巴佬，我的饲养者
痴迷于一种象征游戏游戏里我从手掌上悬挂下来的那
些小趾是猪。还做着典型的猪屎勾当一只小猪去了市
场。 一只嚼着烤牛肉。
从槽里扒出猪饲料，仿佛就是红葱酱里的羊腰
子。当然，我适应，这无形的 加了一点猪肉的化
学物餐食。
吸入谷氨无聊酸钠 听着卡戴珊之流的泪汪汪的尖叫我喜欢这种轰隆隆
的音乐声悲痛的机器果园 我要叫一只猪一只操蛋猪。这个金发的弗朗
茨品种潜进我办公大楼的各个大厅。
他抬起头来张开整个裂腭，使我能看见他那摇动猪鼻子里被微风轻抚的
金黄毛。
发光的白鬼子眼睛。
他舔了舔嘴唇，用眼睛瞄着脊梁骨。热猪油涂在冷的警
棒。野公猪仍然漫游在马林的树林，在奥克兰的街头遍地
是猪。它们对一个收垃圾的人说着难听的话。 我得到一张
罚单，是因为大量倾倒垃圾。那头猪则感谢我，递来复写
页。玷污了我持久的皮肤的亲和力。我抓住他的尾巴，把
它拉得像注射了肉毒杆菌素一样绷紧。那不是 堆肥玷污了
我手指的纹路，猪。
是它贬低了这个美丽的盐渍地我每天穿上衣服：白色但憎恶猪的，充
满着可爱的怨恨。闻起来有点昨天的味道。
新鲜的鱼。大土豆。都扔进
了垃圾箱。干邑白兰地喂了猪。

—translated by Na Ye 娜夜译

猪

我决不会跟猪手拉手。
但是，我的主人迷上了那游戏，
他看我就是个营养不良的乡下人
我不由自主，正扳起了倒悬着的手指头

就是猪了。做着猪的勾当
去市场，吃着烤牛肉。
在食槽边吃出响声，拨出垃圾，像是
红酱里浸着的羊腰子。是的，就是调料，

我给我自己不像样儿的化学晚餐放上
一点猪肉。吸点无聊的结晶体来调味
听见愤怒的卡戴珊做作的尖叫，还眼泪汪汪
多稀罕那受不了的声响
震响了被我丢了的机器果园，
而我要叫一只猪，一只操蛋的猪。
这个金发的德意志
钻进我办公大楼的一个又一个大厅
他抬起头，张开他的裂颚，使我轻易看见
他那摇晃的猪鼻子里正被微风轻拂的金黄体毛
白的眼睛发出斜刺光。
他舔了舔嘴唇，眼睛瞄到了脊梁，热猪油涂上冰冷的
警棍。野猪们还在马林的树丛里自由游逛，但是，奥克兰街头
所有能见到的都是猪。对一个捡垃圾的人
说着令人生厌的猪话。我得到一张罚单，因为滔滔不绝
的倾诉。那头猪准备感谢我，猪手递过来
复写的纸，弄脏了我的这苍老

皮肤的柔光。我抓住他的尾巴，把他拉得
像打了瘦脸针一样紧绷着，那不是

猪粪弄脏了我手指上的皱折，猪。
就是这样污浊了这美丽的盐田
每天我都穿上这一身的白，但是我憎恶猪的行头，
充满着可爱的仇恨。闻起来有昨天的馊味
变质的鱼。大土豆。扔进
垃圾里的东西。快拿酒来请猪们干杯。

—translated by Wang Xiaoni 王小妮译

原诗 Original Poem

CORRESPONDENCES

I don't think language is light
but something sees
through the floating corset
passing through the colon of
this salsa
I chug it with my familiars.

Nothing really resembles anything else
and language is not light.
Hold up this page, you're just trying to
conjugate plastic.
It doesn't. There are sovereigns so fabulous

they delight in roasting children.
A horrible Baudelaireanism to include
in this translation for you
who have just painted a nursery. Did you all
decide on taupe or emerald? Nevermind

they do not delight in roasting children
but rather tomatillos. The whining skins
of peppers. Corn. Corn from
musky, incendiary tubes.

直译 Literal Translation

应和 [1]

我认为语言不是光而是某种看透飘逸的胸衣的东西
穿过莎莎酱的结肠的东西
我跟熟悉的（人）举杯，一饮而尽。

真的没什么酷似任何别的
而语言不是灯光。
拿起这一页，你只是在试图
屈折 [2] 成塑料。
它没有。有些君主如此美妙神奇/像寓言般/传说般/难以置信

他们喜欢/乐于烤烧儿童。
一种可怕的波德莱尔主义 [3] 包括在
为你的这篇翻译中
（你们）刚画完一个托儿所。你们都
决定用灰褐色还是翡翠绿？没关系
他们并不喜欢烤烧儿童
而是粘果酸浆。辣椒唧唧歪歪/抱怨的作响
的皮。玉米。玉米来自
有麝香味的、燃烧着的管子。

注释 Notes & Explanations

1. 《应和》是法国象征派诗人波德莱尔的代表作《恶之花》中的一
篇。

2. 语法的变化和屈折，这里用作动词。
3. 波德莱尔主义来自夏尔·皮埃尔·波德莱尔（Charles Pierre Baudelaire)，法国伟大诗人，象征派诗歌先驱，现代派奠基者，散文诗的鼻祖。代表作包括诗集《恶之花》及散文诗集《巴黎的忧郁》

诗译 Poetic Translations

应和

我觉得语言不是光
是能透过胸衣的什么
能穿过莎莎酱的结肠
被我和熟悉的人，一饮而尽

语言不是灯光
没有别的什么酷似它
翻开一页，你已试图
弯曲成塑料。
但它没有。有些君主像传说，不可信

他们烧烤过儿童
波德莱尔的恶之花
在为你翻译的译文中
刚画完一个托儿所。你们打算
采用灰褐色还是翡翠绿，这重要吗？

他们并不想烧烤儿童
他们是迷恋粘果酸浆。迷恋辣得发烫的
皮，和玉米。玉米在燃烧的
管子中，散着麝香味。

—*translated by Huang Fan 黄梵译*

57

通感

我以为语言不是灯光但它可以穿透人的胸衣
穿透莎莎酱的结肠的东西我
和他们举杯，一饮而尽。

没有任何事物能成为其他的事物
语言不是灯光。
拿起一页纸，你无法将它折叠成塑料。
每个事物有自己的独立性

他们以训斥来烧烤孩子一种可怕的波德莱尔主义
你刚画完一个幼儿园。你们
决定用灰褐色还是翡翠绿？ 没关系

相对于训斥儿童他们更喜欢果酸酱。
在辛辣中哀嚎的辣椒皮，还有烤炉
里烤出的带有麝香味的玉米

—translated by Na Ye 娜夜译

应和

我看语言不是光
而是某种能透视拂动胸衣的物质

穿过莎莎酱的百转愁肠的物质

我跟熟人举杯，一下见底

真的没谁和谁特别相像
而语言不是灯光。
拿起写满了的这一页，你只是想

把它对折，折成塑料。
而它不同意。有些君王在传说里美妙神奇
像寓言一样很难让人相信

他们喜欢烧烤儿童。
一种可怕的波特莱尔主义藏在
给你的这篇翻译中
刚画完一个托儿所，你们都得
选定了用灰褐色，还是翡翠绿？不过，这没关系

其实，他们并不喜欢烧烤儿童
而是鼓弄粘果酸浆。辣椒叽叽歪歪地出声
它的皮，玉米。玉米是
有着麝香味的，燃着了，那管子。

—*translated by Wang Xiaoni 王小妮译*

原诗 Original Poem

Catullus 108
On Which Animals I Concede Which Body Parts

To the greedy vulture soaring above the forests, with their highly corrosive stomach acids capable of digesting hog cholera and botulism, I give you my tongue. There are several colleagues and former lovebirds who, it's true, have treasured various mobilities of that muscle, but upon my death I concede it be cut out and given to vultures. This might be best accomplished by simply leaving my tongue on the forest floor where these raptors are known to hunt. My eyes should be removed and given to ravens, who with their adaptability to a great variety of climates and ecosystems, should be fairly easy to find. You will want to keep the eyes fairly far away from the tongue, so that a vulture doesn't accidentally get one of the eyes too. I should be gutted thoroughly and my offal left in a place where starving dogs can glut their lacks to total satisfaction. As for the rest of my carcass, once the tongue and eyes and intestines have been removed and left in the proper places for the proper animals to feed, this should be given to hungry wolves. Remember a wolf is never a dog.

直译 Literal Translation

卡图卢斯 [1] 108
论我向哪些动物让出我身体的哪些部位

对翱翔在森林上空的贪婪秃鹰，它们具有能够消化猪瘟和肉毒杆菌的高腐蚀性胃酸，我把我的舌头给你。有几个同事和以前的爱情鸟，真的，珍视过那块肌肉的各种移动性/灵活性，但在我死后，我会让它给切出来给秃鹫。做到这一点的最佳办法，就是把我的舌头放在人们知道的这些猛禽常来狩猎的森林空地。我的眼睛应被挖出来给乌鸦，它们对各种各样的气候和生态系统适应力强，应该较容易找到。您要将眼睛放在相当远离舌头的地方，使秃鹫不至于不小心也弄到一只眼睛。我的内脏应全部取出，我的内脏留在饥饿的狗可以变得餍足/完全满意的地方。至于我尸体的其余部分，一旦舌和眼睛和肠子已被取出并留在适当的地方供合适的动物进食之后，就应给饥饿的狼。记住，狼绝不是狗。

译注 Notes & Explanations

1. 卡图卢斯（Gaius Valerius Catullus），古罗马诗人，生于山南高卢的维罗纳。在奥古斯都时期，卡图卢斯享有盛名，后来慢慢被湮没。他的父亲是尤利乌斯·凯撒的追随者。关于卡图卢斯生平的记载，是由中世纪时零星的记载、与他同时期的作家以及他本人的作品包含的信息拼凑而成。因此，他的生卒年至今不能确定。卡图卢斯的诗歌被其他的诗人广为借鉴。

诗译 Poetic Translations

卡图卢斯 108
论我会向哪些动物出让我身体的哪些部位？

贪婪的秃鹰啊，你喜欢在森林上空翱翔，你的胃酸有能力消化猪瘟，消化肉毒杆菌，我愿意把舌头留给你。从前的同事就是从前的爱情鸟，他们欣赏灵动的肌肉，但我死后，会把它们切下，抛给秃鹰。如何做得更好呢？只要把我的舌头，放到猛禽狩猎的森林空地。把我的眼珠挖出来，留给乌鸦，它们熟悉气候和生态环境，不难找到眼珠。务必要让眼珠远离舌头，别让秃鹰也弄走一只。内脏当然要全部取出，把它们放在饿狗满意的地方。我尸体的剩余部分，一旦舌、眼珠、肠全部取出，就该扔给饿狼。记住，是狼，绝不是狗。

—translated by Huang Fan 黄梵译

卡图卢斯 108
论我向哪些动物让出我身体的哪些部位

对翱翔在森林上空的贪婪秃鹰，
它们具有能够消化猪瘟和肉毒杆菌的高腐蚀性胃酸，我把我的舌头你。
有几个同行和以前的鹦鹉，真的，珍视过那块肌肉的各种灵活性，
但在我死后，我会切出来给秃鹫。做到这一点的最好办法，就
是把我的舌头放在人们知道的这些猛禽常来狩猎的森林空地。我的眼睛
应被挖出来给乌鸦，它们对各种各样的气候和生态系统适应力强，应该
较容易找到。您要将眼睛放在远离舌头的地方，使秃鹫不至于不小心也
弄到一只眼睛。我的内脏应全部取出，留给饥饿的狗。让他们吃的心满
意足。在我的舌头眼睛和肠子被取出，在适当的地方供合适的动物进食
之后，其余的部分，就分给饥饿的狼。
记住，狼绝不是狗。

—translated by Na Ye 娜夜译

卡图卢斯 108

论我向哪些动物让出我身体的哪些部位

在森林上空翱翔的伺机的秃鹫，能消化一切腐朽的胃，接着吧，我的舌
头。

有几个熟人和就要忘光了的爱情的雀鸟，确实，他们都领教和珍视过那
块最灵活的肌肉

但我死后，我会把它切了扔给秃鹫。最好把我的舌头放在猛禽最常出没
的林间。

我的眼睛应该挖出来给乌鸦，它们适应任何气候和生态，应该能轻易发
现它。

您会想到，眼睛和舌头要离得远一点，不要一不小心就让秃鹫意外得到
一只眼睛。

我的内脏一点不剩，全取出来，留在恶狗喜欢用餐的地方。

舌头眼睛肠子都分给猛禽们以后，我的尸体还能剩下的那点儿，它们就
应该给饿了的狼。

记住，是给狼，绝不给狗。

—translated by Wang Xiaoni 王小妮译

原诗 Original Poem

藕像

——他们消灭不了你

是一种天气，
浑身光溜溜誓言，
贴紧淤泥，
神交多年，于是心怀鬼胎，
发明——开窍人子，
花枝招展，占据以泪洗面的、黑暗自闭，
乱成一片地盘。造桥，
他们让像经过，
几块甜食空中掉下丝绸，
胳膊挎着仙女。

（污泥里的藕幸灾乐祸，因为
　　无用？对我不无自豪的愧疚，
它油然而生。
断。
桥倒塌，价值不菲：
这光溜溜的、喜滋滋的仇恨，
会劈开吻——会做善事：
肌肤之死，身体才有感觉，
胸前一阵风声，
像野兔耳朵对天使上瘾。
断然。绝交于——
某个时代总有某些片段：
一刀两断的夫妇，

彼此占山为像，对偶在精致棺椁，
让时间担心，
不错，
曾祖父老城区滴翠一个人民公园，
用胎儿体温，炒热
　　黑暗子宫，
孕育伟大、黑暗，四脚落地，
雷声隆隆在红唇，
毛发像水渗出。
只有恐惧能够让大无畏还乡。
今年，
不速之客横卧失礼的钢丝床，
有无母性，有无锦被，
盖上挺拔的头脑？
有时候，湿漉漉的钉子一晚做梦，
模仿钉子的灯塔羞愧得
　　死无葬身之地。
离开潮润、絮语，
躲到夫人怀抱铁锈，
观念菜篮子装满不朽食色，
深思在庭院，失足岗位，
像杰作，和糯米社团。
很想在纪录片的屁股上拍一下。
集市中，在打价格战，
因脸谱化获罪，收到病虫害发出的
　　警告，只能赞美
　　吴侬软语的——雪臀——谁热爱骚货，
她，折叠
　　伤荷的流苏两腿，
靠边站，"哗啦"，留学苏维埃轮盘，
唯命是从的地球上转动
　　最早的赌徒，是僧侣，是苦行，

甚至洁癖天鹅也只以癞蛤蟆为食。
从何而来，就这样，
来开花会。

　　（黑藕，白藕。
藕，绝交于藕断丝连，
现在归于无色，
姓名是一种有色金属；
像，在黑暗子宫，
是一种天气如此温柔

　　嫩芽的洞穴里，一个人民公园的黑暗子宫，
睡着熊猫。
建国以来，私有化的藕，
采摘一空，偷香窃玉的相片集，
留下臭水池，命根在世上像一支支钢笔，
全是分类与蜻蜓点右键，
选择格式相似的文本，
粘贴到水莲花乳头，
不幸成为庆典。
锁链跑来换防，"哗啦"，一根稻草运气，
是离开倒霉鸡蛋，去
　　救命。
不过河，断桥上的两地恋，
至今还是妖孽。
旧地重游的未来女人，
根据男性、不可靠手书，以及
　　快乐指数，
造塔。历史不写色情小说，但是
　　是一个妓院无法公开的账目。
　　（谜底市场化。
而
　　藕，你的修道院像机关枪横扫，
圣人影壁上无以复加的千疮百孔，

更改这污秽内部：白色潜艇，
就是畜生也不甘寂寞，
良心尚好巡游，
所以断，断然，断然绝交于
    下注。
藕，你的修道院睡着熊猫。

直译 Literal Translation

The Image/Look of Lotus Root[1]

—they can't vanquish you

Is a kind of weather
The whole body (is) naked/slippery oath,
Stay close to/rooted in the mud,
having been soul mates/communed spiritually for years, finally conceived
    with ghost fetus,
Inventing/illuminating—man's child with many holes/enlightened sons of
    men,
The blossoms and branches are waving/soliciting and stretching out,
occupying the tear bathed, self-closing/autistic darkness, being muddled
into a turf/domain/confusing/messed turf/domain[2], build bridges,
They let the image/look go by,
pieces of desserts fell from the sky the silk
holds the fairy maids in their arms.
    (the lotus roots in the mud gloat, because
    useless? guilt not without pride to me
it emerges/rises spontaneously
Break/broken[3]
The bridge is falling down, the price is dear:
This naked/slippery and joyful hatred
will slice open the lips—will do philanthropy:
upon the death of the skin, the body will recover its feeling
 the sound of a gust of the wind in the chest

Is like the ears of the hares getting addicted to angels being
determined to/resolutely
make a clean break at—
some pieces/traces left from an age in the past:
a divorced couple/a couple cut in two with one slice stroke of a knife[4]
one another occupying the mountain and crowning themselves as images,
    writing
couplets/facing each other in the delicate coffin
letting time worried
right, my great grandfather was greening a park /a park named overflowing
    green[5] in the old town
stir fry/hype up the dark womb
with the temperature of the fetus
conceiving greatness, darkness, standing on four feet
the thunder was rumbling on the red lips
the hair oops like water.
Only fear can make the fearless return to their native land.
This year,
unexpected guests lie across the rude steel bed/steel bed that has lost rules
Is there any maternity, any quilts
that can cover this tall and straight mind? Sometimes the wet nails dream all
    night,
making the towers resembling them ashamed to death
without berry ground.
Leaving dampness, low chattering,
hiding in their wives' bosom and clutching/holding the rust,
baskets of concepts are filled with immortal food and color/sex
deep thinking /meditating in the courtyard, losing footing from their
posts/going astray from their posts
like masterpieces, and sticky rice community
would like to slap the hip of the documentaries,
in the market, fighting the price war,
condemned for stereotyping, receive the warning
by pests, can only praise
the soft Wu dialect's—snow hip—who loves sluts[6],
she, fold

Hurt lotus's[7] fimbuillferous legs,
Stand aside, "crash", Study abroad soviet roulette,
rotating obediently on the earth
        The earliest gamblers, are monks, asceticism,
even the swans with OCD feed on toads only.
From where, come like this
for this meeting of flowers.
        (black lotus roots, white lotus roots
Lotus roots, break up at remaining fibers from their broken parts /lingering
    relations[8]
Now immersed/returned to no color/sex,
names are but non-ferrous metal
Image/like, in the dark womb
Is a weather so gentle,
        the cave of the fresh shoots, a dark womb in
a People's Park,
Pandas sleep in it.
Since the founding of the new country, the lotus of the private ownership
has been harvested/plucked all, the photo album stealing scent and
    jade/beautiful young women[9]
Leaving behind the smelling ponds,
the roots of fate are like pens in the world,
all classifications and dragonflies clicking the right bottom,
choosing the texts of the same format,
pasting them to the water lotus's nipples,
unfortunately becoming a celebration.
Chains come to take shifts, "crash", the fortune of a straw
Is to leave the eggs that hit a bad patch, to
save life.
But river/not crossing the bridge, the long-distance love on the broken
    bridge[10]
are still genies/wicked fairies.
The future women/women who never been here paid another visit,
build towers,
according to men/building foundation on men, the unreliable handwriting and
    Index of happiness.

History does not write risqué novels, but

        Is a brothel a ledger that keep its accounts a secret.

        (the marketization of the answers.)

But

        Lotus root, your cloister is like being shot by machine guns,

thousands of boils and holes that can add no more on the saint's screen wall,

change this filthy interior: white submarine,

even cattle are unwilling to be reduced to loneness/to be kept out of the

    limelight

The conscience is still good for cruises,

so to break, resolutely, to resolutely break up at

        chipping in.

The lotus roots, your monastery sleeps pandas.

译注 Notes & Explanations

1. "The image of Lotus" is a homonym of "idol" in Chinese.

2. 乱成一片地盘, there is some ambiguity on the parts of speech. "乱成一片" can be understood as a verb, hence translated as being muddled into or it can be used as adjective to modify turf, meaning very confusing turf.

3. It is another ambiguity on the parts of speech.

4. The expression is used metaphorically to refer to a couple who broke up and decided not to have anything to do with each other.

5. The word is frequently used in the classical poetry and essays to describe the vigorous and vivid green. Literally, it means that the color of green is overflowing from the plants.

6. Wu dialect is the dialect of Su Zhou, Wu Xi, and several other places, which is known for its soft and musical tones.

7. It is the name of a kind of lotus.

8. A Chinese idiom. A section of arrowroot is separated, but the clinging fiber remains. Even when the lotus root breaks, the fibers still hold together. The idiom is used metaphorically to refer to a kind of relationship, like a lotus root, linked though divided.

9. The expression "scent and jade" is used to refer to beautiful young women.

10. It refers to the Broken Bridge on the White Causeway in Hangzhou's West Lake. In Chinese folklore, "The Tale of White Snake", the

protagonist, an immortal snake who transformed into beautiful women, met her mortal sweetheart, Xu Xian, on the broken bridge.

诗译 Poetic Translations

Image of a Lotus Root

"they cannot defeat you"

A kind of weather.
The whole body's a slippery promise.
Keep your roots in the mud. Soul mates for years,
we finally conceive a ghost-fetus,
shining through many holes in our human child. Blossoms
and branches reaching and waving, fill tear stained, autistic darkness,
swirling the muddied turf to build bridges
that let the image pass by. Pieces of cake
fall from the sky, silk embraces fairy girls.
Lotus roots in the mud exult, because
useless guilt and pride spontaneously rise up
and break. The bridge collapses, so costly:
Slippery and joyous hate will slash your lips open, giving to others:
skin sloughs off, your body regains feeling.
Gusty wind in your chest is like rabbits' ears addicted
to angels, determined to make a clean break
from any trace of the past:
the couple irreconcilably divorces, one,
then the other vying for a position on the mountain,
crowning self as an image, face-to-face, composing poems
in that delicate coffin, allowing time its worry.
Right.
My great grandfather tends a park overflowing
with green in the old town.
Hype up the dark womb with heat from the fetus,
conceiving greatness, darkness, on all fours,
thunder rumbling on red lips, hair, oops, wet.
Only fear recalls the fearless back home.

This year, unexpected guests lie on unmade, steel beds.
Can any mother's quilt cover this high, straight mind?
Sometimes wet nails dream all night,
shaming the towers that resemble them to death,
no berry grounds.
Leaving the dampness, a low chatter,
hiding in their wives' bosoms and gripping the rust,
baskets of ideas filled with food for immortals, colors and sex,
meditating in the courtyard, away from their posts,
like masterpieces, like sticky rice community,
want to slap the butt of documentaries in the marketplace,
protesting price wars, condemned for stereotypes,
warned off by vermin, can only praise the mellifluous
Wu dialect's snow hip, who loves sluts, "her,"
folding the fimbuillferrous tasseled legs of the Hurt Lotus.
Stand aside, "crash," study Russian roulette abroad,
rotating obediently on earth.
The first gamblers were monks, ascetics, even swans
with OCD only ate toads.
Where are you coming from, like this, to meet flowers
(black and white lotus roots)?
The roots shred apart, some threads hold on, still
relating, then submerge, no color, no sex,
names are metal without iron,
The image in a dark womb is weather so gentle,
cave of fresh shoots, shade in the People's Park,
where pandas sleep.
Since the founding of our new nation,
the lotus of private ownership has been plucked;
photo albums counterfeit pretty women,
leaving behind putrid pools; fate's roots are like pens
writing on the world, all categories and dragonflies
clicking the right bottom,
choosing texts with the same format,
pasting them onto lotus nipples and celebrating, unfortunately.
Chains alternate, "crash"; the fate of a straw
is to abandon eggs on a slick patch, to save its life.
Long distance love will not span the Broken Bridge;
there are still wicked fairies.

In the future, women who've never been here return
and build towers upon the foundations of men,
their unfaithful calligraphy, index of happiness.
History doesn't write sexy novels, but
history's a brothel, a ledger of secret accounts,
commodifying the codes.
Yet, lotus root, your cloister is like something machine-gunned.
Thousands of lesions and holes add nothing to a saint's screen.
Transform this filthy interior: a white submarine.
Even cattle desire the spotlight.
Conscience is still good for a cruise to resolutely
shred apart from giving.
Lotus roots, in your monastery the pandas sleep.

—*translated by* 白萱华译 *Mei-mei Berssenbrugge*

The Look of Lotus Root

—they can't vanquish you

The body is weather,
a naked, slippery oath,
rooted, close to the mud.
Soulmates come up with an unborn ghost,
inventive, pierced, the lit up son of man,
blossoms and branches waving, stretching,
holding the tear-bathed hold in darkness,
in a confusion of bridges,
letting the look go by.
Little sweets rain. Silks
hold fairy maids in their arms.
The lotus roots because useless
and quickens, the bridges
falling down. You can't afford to smile
but you can't help but get some. This flaking,
rigid sound in my chest is like
big ears hooked on angels

and too ready to book,
pearl, like we used to
before we broke and came up
the bottom, made it regular
to pose, writing
couplets, letting
staring stay on that frayed
minute, then buried, silas
asylum, aflow like stirring
in the dark inside, that baby
warm in majesty, thunder rumbling on red lips,
oops like water.
Fear is the engine of this roughened notebook.
This year, unexpected guests lay cross the rude steel bed.
The steel bed has no rules.
Is there any maternity, any quilt
To cover these old growth forests?
Sometimes the wet nails dream all night,
making the towers that look like them ashamed
of that low meadow.
Leaving dampness, low chattering,
hiding in their wives' bosom, clutching rust,
baskets of concepts are filled with endless rubs and tastes
in the courtyard, studying, losing footing from their posts
like masterpieces of the sticky rice community.
Wanna slap the hip of the documentaries,
in the market, fighting the price war,
condemned for bad touch, off levels, Wu's soft dialects,
her snow hips, her loved sluts and folds, soft lotus,
big legs? Stand aside, "crash", study soviet roulette abroad,
rotating obediently on the earth
   The earliest gamblers are monks, cool with the poor,
the swans, with OCD, who feed on toads.
Where you come from looking for some flowers?
(Black lotus roots, white lotus roots,
lotus roots broke up in remaining fibers caught up in antichrome
names, just soft metal

in early wind.
The cave of the fresh shoots, our secret garden, our People's
Park for sleeping pandas, our
locus for stolen growing,
till the founders stole our flowers, made pictures of perfume,
scarred, turned our water like it was written,
ill classifications and dragonflies clicking the right bottom,
choosing the texts of the same format,
pasting them to the water lotus's nipples,
unfortunately becoming a celebration.
Chains come to take shifts, "crash." The fortune of a straw
is to leave the eggs that hit a bad patch, to
save life.
But river, the long-distance love on the broken bridge
is still a genie. The women who never been here pay another visit,
build towers out of men and their
unreliable handwriting and
   index of happiness.
History doesn't write risqué novels, but
   it is a brothel,
a ledger with secrets
   (of the marketization of answers.)
But lotus root, your cloister is like being shot by machine guns.
Thousands of boils and holes that can't add no more on the saint screen wall
change this filthy interior. White submarine,
even cows won't be alone.
The conscience is still good for cruises,
so to break, resolutely. To resolutely break up at
   chipping in, so to speak, to resolutely speak—
The lotus roots. Your monkish pandas sleep.

—*translated by* 弗莱德·莫顿译 *Fred Moten*

The Lotus Root Idol:

They can't defeat you

is a kind of weather
Whole body naked ambiguous promise
Keep your roots in the mud
soul mates for years, finally pregnant with a ghost fetus
enlightened discontinuous human child
Leaves and flowers reach out
into the weepy autistic dark
stuck in torn-up circumstances, invent a bridge
They let appearances go
desserts fall from the sky silk threads
cradle the myth maidens because
they're useless, guilt a source of pride
emerging spontaneously
breaking
The expensive bridge is falling down
This slippery happy hatred
will slice lips open, philanthropically:
when the skin is gone, the body recovers feeling
wind gusting in the chest
addicted to transcendence hares prick up their ears
determined absolutely
to completely separate from --
Still a few old things left
The exes make a clean break
living on the mountaintop
exchanging couplets
face to face in their upscale coffins
letting time deal with the consequences
and, sure, my great-grandfather's garden was
the greenest in the village
stir-fry the hype in the dark womb
the temperature of the fetus
suggesting grandeur, darkness standing on all fours

thunder rumbling on ruby lips
the hair -- oops -- like water.
Nothing but fear compels the fearless back home.
This year,
unexpected guests sprawl across the iron bunks not up to code
What mother, what comforter
can soothe the rigid mind?
The damp nails dream obsessively
mortally embarrassing the look-alike towers
leaving surly dampness
muttering under the wife's blouse, clawing the rust,
inboxes stuffed with ambrosia and sex
deep thinking in the courtyard drifting off
masterfully, sticky rice fellowship
wanting to spank the documentaries
fighting the currency wars in the market
guilty of stereotyping, let fleas be a warning
nothing but praise for that soft Wu accent
icy hips slut-loving she
folding the wounded lotus's legs
Stand back -- "Crash." Study
Russian roulette abroad
rotating obediently with the earth
Ascetic monks were the first gamblers
Swans with OCD will only eat toads
Come here
meet the flowers
(black lotus root, white lotus root)
Lotus root, pestle your connecting fibers
no longer a color
names are merely unrusting metal
images in the dark womb
with such lovely weather
cave of fresh sprouts, dark womb
in a People's Park
where pandas sleep
Since the founding of the new country

the lotus of private ownership
has been harvested completely
all the pretty young things
stashed in private catalogs
leaving stinking ponds behind
fate's roots are like holding pens
mere classification
dragonflies clicking on the lower right
each page opening with the same format
pasted onto the nipples of the lotus
going viral, alas
Chains take their shifts, "crash," the straw's fate
is to scatter off the rotten eggs,
a lifesaver
But long distance romance across the broken bridge
always runs into the wicked gnome
The women of the future -- we've never seen them --
build their towers on men's bad handwriting and happiness indexes
History doesn't write erotic fiction, it's a brothel
with a secret ledger
Selected answers can be had for a fee.
Lotus root, your monastery is like machinegun fire
boils and piercings add no lustre to the saint's screen
redo this disgusting interior, white submarine
even the cattle refuse to be isolated
Conscience still permits going on cruises
anything to break, to totally break with routine
Lotus root, pandas doze in your monastery

—translated by 鲍勃·帕里曼译 Bob Perelman

娜达 高登 / Nada Gordon

原诗 Original Poem

My Dexadrine, I Am So Wistful Like Amber in the Rumpus

O starling, say it scratchy to me,
Scratch your lowing hands out beneath the bless of love:
Were there lies on desertion?
Through the screen, I look upon the lies.
My überman, you are so b-rated just like a raging under,
Where all the buds are bound to be humiliated.
One doubt underneath your bootsteps that flustered and fly away,
As your tears had bring the diary into lissome pretension.
I … I will be your thoughts in goats,
Wherever pains are gone and there are smiling motors.

直译 Literal Translation

我的右旋安非他命 ¹，我是多么惆怅像喧嚣中的琥珀

噢燕八哥，说它瘙痒于我/用刮噪的声音/咄咄逼人地跟我说话，
挠你低垂的手伸出于爱的恩泽下：
离弃是否承载谎言？
透过屏幕，我望着谎言。
我的超人 ²，你如此 B 级的/劣等 ³就像下面的怒火，
那儿所有花蕾都注定被侮辱。
一个疑惑在你的靴子脚下慌忙飞走，
你的眼泪已将日记带入柔软的伪装/借口。
我...我将成为山羊中你的思想，痛苦不论在哪里消失都会有微笑的
　　马达。

译注 Notes & Explanations

1. Dexadrine，右旋安非他命，一种兴奋剂

2. überman 或者 *übermensch*，尼采笔下的超人。

3. B 级意思是平庸的、劣等和廉价的。

诗译 Poetic Translations

我的右旋安非他命，我如此渴望像喧嚣中的琥珀

噢燕八哥，用呱噪的声音向我说话，挠着你从爱的恩泽下伸
出的手：离弃中是否藏着谎言？透过屏幕，我盯着它。
我的超人，你拙劣的表演就像地狱之火，在那里所有花蕾都注定被侮辱。
一个疑惑在你的靴子下仓皇飞走，当你的眼泪已将日记带入柔软的伪装。
我——我将成为山羊中你的思想，
痛苦不论去向哪里都会发动微笑的马达。

—translated by Lan Lan 蓝蓝译

我的右旋安非他命，我是多么渴望在喧嚣中安静

噢八哥　你用呱噪的声音和我说话
从在爱的祝福之下　挠着你低垂的手：
离弃之中是否有谎言？透过屏幕
我望着这谎言
我的超人，你的愤怒如此低劣
让花蕾般的女人遭受侮辱
你脚下的疑问慌不择路
当你的眼泪将日志伪装的柔软
我……我不过是你意淫的想法
痛苦一消失就会有微笑的马达轰鸣。

—translated by Na Ye 娜夜译

79

我的右旋安非他命，我像喧嚣中的琥珀神伤心渴

噢，燕八哥，用聒声刮我，
从爱的恩佑下抓挠出你低垂的双手：
离弃中藏有谎言？
透过屏幕，我望着谎言。
我的超人，你如此烂俗就像下面的暴狂，
那儿所有的花蕾都注定被侮辱。
一个疑惑自你靴底慌忙飞走，
当你的眼泪已将日记带入优雅的做作。
我.....我将成为山羊中你的心思，
不论痛苦去向何方都会有微笑的马达。

—translated by Xi Chuan 西川译

原诗 Original Poem

Whenever I Waver Between Two Rathers

Whenever I wither between two reality shows
I see beautiful green goddesses along the way.
Its lighten up by the tulips.
I ask myself, "Is this my crybaby?"
Whenever the wincing left me behind.
All just a open blur to a storm that zithered
Mein kopf, wishing you are helium with me.
Hear! The crickets are dreaming to say love.
Please, don't libel me,
Hold my ideas and you'll see the petulance of life with me

直译 Literal Translation

无论何时我摇摆在两种或许中

每当我在两种真人秀中枯萎
我沿路看见美丽的绿色女神。
它被郁金香点亮。
我问我自己："这是我爱哭的宝贝/鼻涕虫么？"
每当畏缩将我遗弃。
一切只是一朵盛开的污迹之于一场风暴的拨弄/一切只是向暴风雨敞开
　　的一块模糊，被齐特拉琴一样弹拨[1]
Mein kopf[2]，愿你于我是氦气。
听着！蟋蟀正在做梦/梦中表达爱意。
请，不要诋毁我，
握住我的思想，
你将和我一起看见生活焦虑的性子。

译注 Notes & Explanations

1. Zither, 齐特琴，一种古代的拨弦乐器。
2. Mein kopf: 这是对希特勒的《我的奋斗》的一个戏仿。德语中"我的
　　奋斗"为 "Mein Kampf'，而这里的 "Kopf"是"头"的意思。由于英
　　文中保留德文，此处亦保留德文。

诗译 Poetic Translations

每当我摇摆在两种或许中

每当我在两种真人秀中枯萎沿途就能看见美丽的
绿女神。祂被郁金香点亮。
我自问："这是我爱哭的鼻涕虫吗？" ——每当畏缩让我退后。
一切只是暴风雨中敞开的迷雾，被那齐特拉琴一样地弹拨着的

Mein kopf，愿你于我是氢气。听！蟋蟀在梦中表达爱意。
请不要诋毁我，握住我的思想，你将看见我生活中的焦灼。

—*translated by Lan Lan* 蓝蓝译

每当我在两种可能中动摇

当我在一场真人秀的表演中枯萎就看见被
郁金香点亮的绿色女神向我走来我问自
己："这是我爱哭的宝贝吗？" 每当我退
缩。
一切只是暴风雨中模糊的风景，被齐特拉琴弹拨我的头，愿你于我是氢
气。听！蟋蟀在梦中表白着爱。请不要诋毁我，握住我的思想，你就看
见生活中焦虑的我。

—*translated by Na Ye* 娜夜译

每当我摇摆在两种或许中

每当我在两个真景秀中枯萎我沿路看见美丽的绿色女神。
它被郁金香点亮。
每当我畏葸不前
我便自问："这是我的鼻涕眼泪虫吗？"
一切只是一块污迹敞向被奏响的风暴
Mein kopf（我的奋头），愿你是我的氢气。
听！蟋蟀梦想着说爱。
请，不要中伤我，
攥住我的想法，你将看到我的急脾气。

—*translated by Xi Chuan* 西川译

原诗 Original Poem

I Need Your Prurient Lantern

When the noxiousness lie down beside me,
When the meek and staring are shimmying brightly,
You'll make my lines become so lovely,
A gargoyle of love poems that I adore.
Don't you know that I am a 'pataphysicist?
Really, I need your prurient lantern,
To pacify me from your mishearings,
And glide me to be your santa of love,
Show me the weirdness,
Prove me for your energetic lilt.
By the time I try,
To call your narrative with one and only loudness through me.

直译 Literal Translation

我需要你欲望的灯笼

当毒性在我身旁躺下，
当温顺和凝望的人明亮地摇动，
你将使我的线条变得如此可爱，
一个我珍爱的情诗的滴水嘴/怪兽雕塑。
难道你不知我是一个"超然玄学家"[1]？
真的，我需要你欲望的灯笼，
使我从你的误听里平息，
然后让我滑入你爱情的圣诞老人，
将诡谲展现给我，
证明我为你那激情/活跃的调子/歌喉。
当我尝试，
呼唤你的故事通过一个和唯一一个穿过我的巨响。

译注 Notes & Explanations

1. Pataphysics: 荒诞玄学/后形而上玄学/超然科学，是一种对幻想及不存在的问题的荒诞式的解答。这个词是法国作家阿尔弗雷德·雅里臆造出来的。

诗译 Poetic Translations

我需要你好色的灯笼

当这剧毒在我身旁躺下，
当温顺和凝望明亮地摇动，
你将使我的线条变得如此可爱，
一尊我珍爱的兽头滴水嘴流下情诗。
难道你不知我是一个"后形而上玄学家"？
是的，我需要你好色的灯笼，
使我从你的误听里平息
以拒绝它然后让我滑入你爱情的圣诞老人
的身体，将诡谲展现给我，
为我证明你那激情音调的歌喉 。
当我尝试，
呼唤你的故事，通过唯一的一个穿越我的巨响。

—*translated by Lan Lan* 蓝蓝译

我需要你淫荡的灯笼

它带着毒性躺在我身边，当温顺的绒毛竖立
明亮而快乐地震颤，它使我身体的线条无比生动，
我崇拜的　　爱情诗的怪兽滴水嘴。
难道你不知道我是一个"荒诞玄学家"？是的，我需要你淫荡的
灯笼，抚慰我　　使我滑翔着成为你爱情的圣诞老人，省略语言的误
解　　将你的诡谲展现给我，向我证明你雄性的充满活力的激情。

现在我开始尝试，
用那唯一的一次穿过我身体的巨响　　召唤你。

—translated by Na Ye 娜夜译

我需要你淫色的灯笼

当毒性躺到我身旁，当温顺和凝视明亮地颤动，你会将我的线条变得如此可爱，变成我慕爱的注水兽头口吐情诗。难道你不知我是"荒诞玄学家？真的，我需要你淫色的灯笼，使我得以从你的误听里平复，使我滑向你，变成你的圣诞爱人，让我看到怪异，以你激情的快动作给我证明 。
当我试着做，
唯一的大声吟讶穿透我，呼唤你的故事。

—translated by Xi Chuan 西川译

Huang Fan / 黄梵

原诗 Original Poem

蝙蝠

蝙蝠在这里，那里
头顶上无数个黑影叠加
顷刻间，我的孤独有了边界

假如我浮上去
和它们一起沐浴
我会成为晚霞难以承受的惊人重压

当蝙蝠慢慢拖动霞光
我孤独着，蝙蝠便是我的黑天鹅
无数尖齿鸣叫着催促我的血流

一圈又一圈
它们幸福的希望在哪里？
还是每只蝙蝠都想试用月亮这块滑板？

我开始感到它们振翅的温暖
蝙蝠，害怕孤独的蝙蝠，也许你我错在——
不能交谈，却如此接近

直译 Literal Translation

Bats

Bats here, there
Countless black shadows above the crown of the head/overhead overlap In an
instant/Instantaneously, my loneliness has gotten/has found a boundary/a
border
If I float up
Immerse myself among them/To bathe with them
I will become the sunset glow's/sunset clouds' unbearable, astonishing
pressure/heavy load
When the bats' slowly drag the multicolored sunset light
I'm lonely/solitary, bats are just like/are precisely my black swans
Countless pointed/sharp teeth sound/shriek, urging/stimulating my blood
Circle/loop after circle/loop
Where are their wishes/hopes for happiness?
Or does each bat want to try out the moon, this skateboard?
I begin to feel the warmth of their beating/flapping wings
Bats, loneliness-fearing bats, maybe our/your and my mistake is/lies in—
Can't/Shouldn't/Inability to converse/talk/discuss, even if so close/but in this
way/thereby approach/get close

译注 Notes & Explanations
1. "drag" as in "drag a computer mouse"

诗译 Poetic Translations

Bats

Bats everywhere—
The sky wearing a wig of bats.
My loneliness
has found its upper limit.
If I float up to join them,

I'll be crushed in sunset's
astonishing weight. But
when bats drag away that
luminous cursor, I'm
bereft.
Then their squeals
come back for me.
What are they after?
The bats do loop de loops.
Do they want to ride the moon—
that skateboard?
They get my blood up.
More than anything,
the bats hate loneliness.
If we'd learned to converse, we
might be close like that.

—translated by 雷伊·艾尔曼特罗特译 Rae Armantrout

Bats

Huang Fan I hope you will
not be offended that I am
using the occasion of reading
your poem "Bats" to share
that I just learned the most
unbelievable thing about the
soundtrack to *Batman* (1989,
dir. Tim Burton) starring
Michael Keaton, Jack Nicholson
and Kim Basinger which is
that while it is well known that
the soundtrack was written
and recorded by Prince, featuring
what has to be one of the
strangest number one pop

hits every recorded, "Batdance,"
a tune which is really less of
a pop song than a medley of
Prince's musical ideas at the
time, I would say "miniature
Vermeers" but that is of course
redundant, bricolaged together
in a fairly chaotic sequence
tied together by solo guitar
and samples from the film,
what is less well known is that
the plan for the soundtrack
originally was for it to be a
collaboration between Prince
and Michael Jackson where
Prince would sing the funky
songs and Jackson all the
slow ones, can you even
believe that this was almost
an object in our world?

—translated by 布兰登 布朗译 Brandon Brown

Bats

Bats here, there, uncountable shadow and ceiling. Now, my
loneliness has a border. If I float up to bathe with them I'll be
that pressure on the sun when they drag colored light across.
I'm lonely and bats are my black swans, my blood uncountably
soundpierced loop by loop. Are their wishes lost or do they want
to acid drop the moon? Their friction sings, is scared to be alone,
and we're not even close enough to talk.

—translated by 弗雷德·莫顿译 Fred Moten

原诗 Original Poem

偶遇故人

突然间，我听见熟人的喊声
他的脸像蝙蝠，在黑暗中低飞
他的眼里，已看不见年轻时的爱情

他一路咳过来，仿佛要阻止雾霾
"雾霾里有骨头"，他说
"你摸不着，但能卡住喉咙"。
是啊，雾霾加重了往日的幸福
可令我们贬值的，是年龄，被洗劫一空的年龄啊

他伸出手，又缩回去
我的手，只抓住了哄抬物价的夜色
当他胡言乱语，唉，又一出泪光莹莹的悲剧——
他病得多么卓尔不群啊！

断了多年的友情
却得用一路的痛缝上
这痛让我变笨，撞到路边的树干
这痛不善言辞，把黑夜的黑发，熬成黎明的白发

上午，当太阳抛弃朝霞这幅名画
悄悄爱上云层的鱼尾纹
它仿佛说："孩子，我最终也会烧成废铁。"
我一赌气，把被子晒出去
等着睡前闻到阳光的气味

直译 Literal Translation

Running Into An Old Friend

All of a sudden/Suddenly, I hear the shout of a familiar person
His face is like a bat, flying low in the night sky
In his eyes, youth's love is already invisible
He coughs the whole way over, as if to block the smog

"The smog has bones/In the smog are bones," he says
"That you can't touch, but that can jam/choke/catch in your throat."
Ah yes/Yes/Indeed, the smog weighs down the past's happiness
Can make us/cause us to/order us to devalue/depreciate, it's age, ah it's the
looted-bare/plundered/emptied age

He extends his hand, and withdraws it/retrieves it/pulls it back My
hand only catches the driven up/artificially inflated dusk light/dim
evening light
While he babbles nonsense, alas, there occurs a tear-glistening tragedy/a
tragedy glistening with teardrops—
Ah, he's sickened into something exceptional!

The friendship's been broken off/cut off for many years
But/Yet we can use the whole journey's/the whole time's pain/sadness to sew
it up/stitch it up/it will have to be sewn up with the entire journey's pain This
pain/sickness/disease has made me stupid/has dumbed me/has made me
foolish, running into/bumping into a roadside/curbside tree trunk
This pain/sickness/disease isn't articulate, makes the night's black hair
cooked into/stewed into/boiled into the dawn's white/gray hair Morning,
when the sun abandons/discards/casts aside/forsakes the famous painting of
rosy dawn

Quietly/Secretly/Covertly falls in love with the cloud strata's wrinkles
It seems to say: "Child, in the end I'll also be burned/melted into scrap
metal/scrap iron."

In an angry reaction/As soon as I act rashly out of a feeling of being
wronged, I set the quilt out to sun/to bask in the sun Waiting until
just before sleep to smell the scent of sunlight

译注 Notes & Explanations
1. "artificially inflated" is an economic term
2. "babbles nonsense" is idiomatic
3. "alas" is an interjection equivalent to a sigh
4. the clause "there occurs a tear-glistening tragedy/there occurs a tragedy
    glistening with teardrops" is preceded by an adverb that can indicate "and
    yet" / "also" / "simultaneously"

诗译 Poetic Translations

Running Into An Old Friend

Out of nowhere, I think I hear him again,
and there's his bat-face, swooping towards me.
In his eyes, young love is extinguished.

He covers his cough, like it's nothing,
hacking up this smog. He says, "The smog has bones.
They stick in your craw."
"Past happiness depreciates like an old car."
Did he always talk such nonsense?
Perhaps he has sickened
into something extraordinary?

Disease has made me dumb.
I think maybe we can patch things up, but, in the morning,
the sun doesn't even try its old "rosy fingered dawn" routine.

As it heats up, it yells that it too is being melted down
for scrap metal.

Defiantly, I set my quilt out anyway
—to bask!

Later, in the dark, it gives off
a familiar whiff of light.

—*translated by* 雷伊 艾尔曼特罗特译 *Rae Armantrout*

Stop and Chat

This poem by Huang Fan
"Running Into An Old Friend"
tells an anecdote of the poet
walking in the dark and
hearing the shout of someone
familiar. An old friend who
speaks in prosodic riddles
like *The smog has bones /*
Inside the smog is just bones.
He teases the poet with a
fake handshake, looks extremely
sick, and you can tell the
poet sort of hates this "friend"
and really wishes he had
not run into him. Except that
it became the occasion for
a poem. And when the poem
comes you can't, or at least
shouldn't, repeal it from the
legislature of your own fantasies.
I don't know Huang Fan or
his friends. All I have is poetry
and a couple of thousand
dollars, my heart, my
beautiful friends who I want to see
all the time except for the times

when I do not no matter how
heavy their beauty. Sometimes
my bones are full of smog
which is not the time for
a stop and chat beyond
the exchange of pleasantries
which of course are
degraded in all the poems

of all the world's languages
but still are technically pleasant.

—translated by 布兰登 布朗译 Brandon Brown

Running Into an Old Friend

Suddenly, I know that voice,
the bounced-off presence of
old-face Andre in the dark,
repurposing the creamy air.

We breathing sticks you can't
feel, he says. Feel the splinters
in your throat? I can't remember
what we used to be worth.

He held his hand out just to leave
me grasping speculative twilight,
but that mess he was breathing,
his breath all short, was shining.

We'd been cut off for years but
that whole sad way sewed us up
again. We'd been mute as what
mutes us, this inarticulate gray,

till that burst and rose collision
and that angry patch of sun.

—translated by 弗雷德 莫顿译 Fred Moten

原诗 Original Poem

蒸汽火车

用蒸汽，与乡村的炊烟握手
用铁轨，铺出远方清冷的夜色
分手的伤痛，终于找到铁轨这张世上最长的床
轮子的昼夜响动，奏出世上最优雅的痛

他不知万里之外雪的寂静
已像方言，正被官话融化
从此，他每年用生日这枚钉子
钉住漂泊的人生，如同背包客
用车站这把钉子，钉住乱世的风景

铁轨已是祖国这片叶子上清晰的叶脉
把人流像泪水，送进每个受伤的村庄
火车也是长蛇，小心穿过雪山的白大褂
避免与雪崩一起合唱
它更是扩阴器，扩开了双乳峰的下体
四周站满不说话的雪山大夫

他像火车体内异位的胎儿
始终不肯下车出世
直到挂满天空的星星露珠
擦亮月光这把银刀，剖开它的肚子

重新上路的火车，失望地朝戈壁吐着烟圈
他像蒸汽，开始踮起脚尖向家乡眺望——
挥手告别的蒸汽啊，至多能遮住悲剧
但不能避免悲剧

直译 Literal Translation

Steam Train/Steam Engine

Use/With steam, to shake hands with smoke from the village chimneys/rural cooking
Use/With railroad tracks, to lay out/spread out/extend the distant, desolate dusklight/evening light
The grief of parting, at last/finally finds the railroad track, this longest bed on Earth/in the world
The wheels' day-and-night/round-the-clock sound/churning with sound plays out the Earth's/world's most elegant/graceful pain/sorrow/ache

He doesn't know/He is unaware of the faraway snow's quiet/the tranquility of snow that's ten thousand *li* away
Already like (a) dialect(s), now being melted/dissolved by Mandarin/the official language
From now on/Whence, each year he uses the (powerful/authoritative) nail of his birthday
To nail down drifting/wandering life, like a backpacker Using the handful of nails of the railroad station, to nail down the chaotic/turbulent world's scenery/landscape

Railroad tracks are already the distinct/clear veins on this leaf
the homeland is
Sending/Delivering/Carrying people, like teardrops, to every injured/wounded village
The train is also a long snake, carefully crossing/passing through the snowy peaks' long white gowns

96

To avoid joining the avalanche's chorus
It's even more a Yin-/sexual organ-/genitals-enhancing/magnifying tool,
enlarging the twin-peak mountain/breast-peaks' nether regions/lower part
Around stand (a crowd of) silent Doctor Snow Mountains/doctors that the
snow peaks are

He is like a wrongly-positioned fetus/embryo (lodged) inside the train body
Unwilling all along to disembark and be born/appear/emerge in the world
Until the night is hung full of dewdrop stars
Polishing the moon, this silver blade/knife, cutting open its
belly/abdomen/stomach

The train once again beginning its journey/Once again on the road, the train
disappointedly/despairingly spits smoke rings at the Gobi
He's like steam, beginning to rise onto tiptoes to see/to look afar for his
hometown—
Ah, the steam waving goodbye can at most cover up tragedy
But can't avert/prevent/avoid tragedy

译注 Notes & Explanations

1. In stanza 1/line 3: the metaphor compares the railroad tracks to the longest bed on Earth.
2. In stanza 1/line 4: "plays out" as in 'plays music.'
3. In stanza 2/line 1: one *li* equals half a kilometer.
4. In stanza 3/line 1: the metaphor compares the homeland to a leaf and the railroad tracks to veins on that leaf.
5. In stanza 3, line 5: 扩阴器, pronounced in Chinese Pin Yin as " kuo yin qi", is a coinage by the poet that originates from the homonym 扩音器 （megaphone/sound magnifying device). It has been literally translated here as "Yin-/sexual organ-/genitals-enhancing tool".
6. In stanza 3/line 5, "nether regions/lower part" is a euphemism for female genitalia.

诗译 Poetic Translations

Steam Engine

Use steam to shake hands with the village cooking fires.
Use tracks to spread the desolate evening light.
The grief of parting belongs to this track, the longest bed on earth.
The wheels' arpeggio produces the world's most elegant headache.

He doesn't even know about snow's silence five thousand miles away
and already like a dialect being absorbed into the language of officials.
From now on he will use the spike of each birthday
to fasten his life to these tracks,
to hold down the messy landscape.
Railroad tracks are already raised veins on this country,
bringing people, like tears, to the wounded towns.
And the train is now a long snake, sliding between
the white dresses of the mountains
or it's an amped up vagina, engorging the world's
nether regions while a gaggle of snow-capped doctors
looks on.

He must be an awkward fetus, lodged in the train's
body, unwilling to be born — unless the moon's
sickle cuts him free.

Once again moving, the train blows smoke rings
at the Gobi. He's like steam rising
to see his hometown from afar.
Steam will cover disaster,
but nothing can stop it.

—translated by 雷伊 艾尔曼特罗特译 *Rae Armantrout*

Steam Train Steam Engine

I keep misreading this line
in Huang Fan's poem
"Steam Train" which might
also be translated as "Steam
Engine." Whoever has
literally translated the poem
for me, since I do not know
Chinese, has rendered
the opening of the third
line of the poem as
"the grief of parting at last"
but I keep reading it as
"the grief of partying at last"
which reminds me that
Steve, who quit partying,
and I made plans to go see
some of the punk shows
in the *All's Still Not Quiet On The
Western Front* festival this

year and Steve said let's get
our mid-life crises properly
started. Like a railroad track
facilitates the movement
of long trains, carrying bodies
"like teardrops" "to the injured
villages" the train "is like a snake"
"carefully crossing snowy peaks"
a big nasty smoking snake
full of bodies trying to find
somebody to "bite" like "silent
Doctor Snow mountains"

goodbye steam, goodbye tragedy
goodbye life. Hello imperative
mood. Oh hello tragedy.

—*translated by 布兰登 布朗译 Brandon Brown*

Steam Engine

With steam, he greets the smoke from village chimneys. With tracks, he
spreads the distance. Sad distance lays down tracks and parting makes the
tracks an endless bed. The earth's a flower bed of elegant sadness every
hour.

He can't hear the snow, quiet in an old language, melting in official sun.
The snow is five thousand miles away. His birthday nails the world's landscape
to time.

The tracks are clear veins on a leaf. People are sent like teardrops to every
wounded village. The train bleeds through mountains, threads and snakes
through avalanche and echo, through the mutant wombs and snowbreasts
of the midwife mountains, who are stunned by the breech the train bears.
Nobody wants to get off till night hangs diamond and the moon is polished.
Cut open,

the train
spits and cries sad circles through the Gobi. Like steam, he rises up
to see his home. As steam, he covers up the dead arrival.

—*translated by 弗雷德 莫顿译 Fred Moten*

原诗 Original Poem

变化

光线改变了物体犹如你改变了我
此刻，出现了阴影、曲线
而从前我不知道

这些是我的影子！我运动的面孔
流星、草叶和石上的青苔
众多亲眷　　　系在我身
上的细线——　你的爱与它
们相等你明了这些——　我
世界的幸福与不幸一颗砝
码　　　与一架天平

直译 Literal Translation

Change

Light rays changed/have changed an object
Similar to/Just as how you changed/how you've changed me
Now/At this moment, there appears/emerges/has/have emerged a
        shadow/shadows, a contour/contours
But in the past I didn't know

These are my shadows! My
        movements' faces
Meteor/Meteors, grass blades and moss on rocks
Numerous relatives   connected/bound/tied in

101

The string/thread on my body—
Your love is equal to/is equivalent to theirs
You understand these—
My   world's happiness/fortune and unhappiness/misfortune
A standard weight[1]   and a set of scales

译注 Notes & Explanations
1.   "A standard weight" as in one used on a balance scale

诗译 Poetic Translations

Change

Light changes an object, as you changed me. Now,
a shadow appears, a contour I didn't know.
They're my shadows! My changing expressions—
meteor, grass blade, moss on stones,
so many relatives entwined in my body. Your love
equals theirs. You understand that my great happiness
and unhappiness are: a weight and a set of scales.

—*translated by* 白萱华译 *Mei-mei Berssenbrugge*

Change

Light changes an object
as you changed me.

Now there are shadows
I hadn't seen before

and they're my shadows.
My moving faces. My meteors.

Grass blades.
Moss on rocks.

All my relatives
threaded through my body.

You understand my world,
 its fortune and misfortune:

A standard weight
and a set of scales.

—translated by 娜达·高登译 Nada Gordon

Change

Objects change under bright light
like you've changed me
There are shadows now
I never saw before

It's me casting these shadows!
Meteors, grass blades, a mossy rock
are my expressions
entwined   braided into
a belt around my body
but your love is more specific
You understand
my bliss my misery
An exact   scale

—translated by 鲍勃·帕里曼译 Bob Perelman

原诗 Original Poem

遗失

一个人遗失在信中，书中。
遗失在手离开后的灰尘里
以及椅子 灯光后
被用过的感情的轭具
以及列车呼啸而过的阴影——
他有着树叶和云彩的形状
在他的脚印里
有着积水映出的四季的形状

有时，某人会带着他
在沉重发炎的膝关节里——
走向郊外 就铁轨旁
在一丛被压倒的野蒿上
与另一个他相遇——

一个人遗失在被他遗失的
一切事物中。

直译 Literal Translation

Lost

A person is lost in a letter, a book.
Lost in the dust the departed hand leaves/becomes
As well as that behind the chair   the light/lighting
The yoke of the used emotion
As well as the shadow of the train whistling past/hurtling by—

He has the form of/He's shaped like tree leaves and clouds/colorful clouds
In his footprints
Pooled water reflects the form of the four seasons

Sometimes, a certain person will wear/carry/take   him in
A severely inflamed knee joint—
Walking towards the outskirts   just beside the train tracks
Upon a pressed-down/an overwhelmed/overpowered thicket of wormwood
With another he meets—

A person is lost in the midst of/in the center of
everything he loses/has lost.

诗译 Poetic Translations

Lost

A person gets lost in a letter, a book
In dust the withdrawing hand will become
And the chair and behind the light
And in the yoke of spent emotion
In the shadow of a train speeding by—-

His form is like foliage and colored clouds
In his footprints
pools of water reflect the forms of all seasons
Sometimes, a certain person will carry him
With his badly swollen knee
Walking to the edge of town along train tracks
Over a crushed thicket of wormwood
And meet another person—-
A person lost in the midst of everything he is losing.

—translated by 白萱华译 Mei-mei Berssenbrugge

Lust

(after Lan Lan's "Lost")

A person lusts in letters, in books.
Lusty and dusty the hand withdraws
becoming a backlit sex swing.

Used emotion is a joke
like the shadow of the hurtling A train
on the wall of the cave.

He is momiji and psychedelic clouds
And in the wet pools of his footprints
are reflected Viewmasters ™ of the Four Seasons

Sometimes specific people carry him
in their inflamed knees, walking their fingers
under skirts, meeting The Other
on the wrong side of the tracks,
overwhelmed in a thicket
of wormwood.

A person is lost
in the center of everything
she lusts for.

—translated by 娜达·高登译 Nada Gordon

Lost

Someone gets lost in a letter, a book
gets lost in the dust the absent hand leaves
gets lost in his chair, the light behind it
the straightjacket of superceded feelings
plus the train's shadow whooshing by

He looks like a leaf, a sunset cloud
Water pools in his footprints
reflecting each season in turn
Sometimes someone with bad knees
carries him to the outskirts
Between the tracks and a ratty thicket
of wormwood he meets --

Someone gets lost in the middle
of his losses

—translated by 鲍勃·帕里曼译 Bob Perelman

原诗 Original Poem

几粒沙子

1
人们不会询问泪水。他们倾向于带来
平面的事物。在那上面有着被黑布覆盖着的
鹅卵石面包。

不幸不属于大众。那最个人
的仍然是一个吻在离开它热爱的花朵时
滴下血，增添了世界的鲜艳。

2
武器。矿难。欣欣向荣的房地产。
各占据一块版面。

其中的炸弹碎片里逃出一只活鸟
在和平国度的窗外击中一个诗人的昏迷

它的深洞，它眼睛里的黑。

3

有时候我忽然不懂我的馒头我的米和书架上的灰尘。

我跪下。我的自大弯曲。

4

树叶飘落。豆子被收割。
泥土在拖拉机的犁头后面醒来。

它们放出河流和风在新的旷野上。

5

我们自身的脚镣成就我们的自由
借助时间那痛楚的铁锤。

6

所有掷向他人的石块都落到我们自己的头顶。

干渴的人，我的杯子是你的你
更早地赐予我有源头的水。

7

幸福的筛子不漏下一颗微尘。不漏下叹息、星光、厨房的炊烟也不
漏下邻居的争吵、废纸、无用的茫然。

除了一个又一个清晨。黄昏。

直译 Literal Translation

A Few Grains of Sand

1

People won't ask about/inquire into tears. They prefer/tend to bring
   about/produce

a flat thing/flat things. On top of it, are pebbles of bread/bread
        crumbs/pebbled-shaped bread
covered by black cloth

Misfortune/Adversity doesn't belong to/isn't a part of the masses. The most
        individualized/independent
is still a kiss that, when it leaves the flower that it loves/is still one who, when
        kissing goodbye its adored flower,
sheds blood, adding to/increasing the world's bright colors/splendor.
 2
Weapons/Arms. Mining disaster. Thriving real estate.
Each occupies/takes up a whole page.
From among these bomb shards/fragments, a living bird escapes
Outside the window of a peaceful country, strikes a poet's stupor/coma

Its deep cave/hole/zero, its eye's black/its pupil/the blackness in its eyes.
 3
Sometimes I suddenly don't understand my steamed bun
My rice and the dust atop the bookshelf.

I kneel down. My arrogance bends/warps.
 4
Tree leaves float down/fall gently/fly down. Beans have been harvested.
The soil awakens behind the plow of the tractor.

They let off/give off river breezes on the new wilderness.
 5
Our own fetters achieve/accomplish our freedom
with the help of time, that painful/anguishing iron hammer.
 6
All the stones thrown at others drop onto our own heads.

Thirsty person, my cup is yours
Earlier you granted me water with a source.
 7
The happy/blessed/fortunate sieve doesn't leak a speck of dust.

Doesn't leak a sigh, starlight, kitchen smoke
and doesn't leak neighbors' quarrels, wastepaper, useless/worthless vacancy.

Except for one and another dawn. Dusk.

诗译 Poetic Translations

A Few Grains of Sand

1
People don't ask about tears. They like to make flat things.
On top are rolled pebbles of bread covered with black cloth.
Trouble's not solely owned by the masses. The most individual,
is the one who kisses the beloved flower goodbye,
and bleeds and increases the world's colors.

2
Arms race, mine collapse, real estate bubble take a whole page each.
Out of the shrapnel, a bird flies.
The poet's muteness strikes at a window in peaceful country.

A deep cave is the black of its eye.

3
Sometimes, I can't understand my steamed bun or rice or dust on the
bookshelf.
I kneel. My pride warps.

4
Leaves from trees flutter down. Beans are harvested.
Soil awakens after the tractor passes by,
Wafting river breezes across a new wilderness.

5
Our own shackles will gain us freedom
with the aid of time, that bludgeoning hammer.

6

Stones I throw at them fall on my own head.
Thirsty friend, I give you my cup.
You gave me water from the source.

7

This lucky sieve won't leak one speck of dust,
not a sigh, not starlight, kitchen smoke, not neighbors' quarrels,
wastepaper, useless blankness,
except each and the other other: Dawn. Dusk.

—*translated by* 白萱华译 *Mei-mei Berssenbrugge*

A Few Grains of Sand

1

People don't ask about tears.
They prefer 2D things.
A black cloth covers
the pebble-shaped breads.

Adversity isn't a mass phenomenon.
An individual is still a kiss that,
when leaving its adored blossom,
sheds blood, increasing
the world's vividness.

2

Weapons. Mining Disaster. Thriving real estate.

Each occupies a whole page.

Out of these bomb fragments
a living bird escapes
leaving the window of a peaceful country
and striking a poet into a coma.

The bird is a deep cave.
Its eyes are dizzying blackness.

3
Sometimes I'm suddenly confused
by my steamed bun,
my rice, and the dust
atop the bookshelf.

I kneel down.

My arrogance warps.

4
Leaves flutter down.

Beans have been harvested.
The soil's been awakened
by the tractor's plough.

5
Our own fetters, with the help of time
achieve for us our freedom.

That excruciating iron hammer.

6
All the stones thrown at others
drop onto our own heads.

O thirsty man – take my cup.
Earlier you gave me spring water.

7
The fortunate sieve doesn't leak
a speck of dust

Doesn't leak a sigh, starlight, kitchen smoke

    or

neighbors' quarrels,
or

wastepaper.

It's a worthless vacancy
except for dawn.

Except for dusk.

—*translated by 娜达·高登译 Nada Gordon*

A Few Grains of Sand

1
People don't care about grief. They prefer
numbness. With crumbs on top
covered by black cloth.

The masses don't care about tragedy. The individual
is a kiss drawing blood from a flower
adding color to the world.

2
Weapon Sales. Mining Disaster. Real Estate Boom.
A whole page for each.

A bird escapes from this shrapnel
flying into the countryside

smacking the dozing poet right in the pupil.

3
And now I don't recognize my lunch
the rice the dust on top of the bookshelf.

I kneel. My arrogance evaporates.
4
The leaves float down. The soybean harvest is in.
Stirred by the tractor the soil awakens

evoking rivers and inconstant winds in the woods.

5
Our chains give us freedom
sealed by time's iron hammer.

6
The stones we throw at others hit us in the head.

Thirsty man, here's my cup.
You showed me where the water was.

7
The lucky sieve never leaks a speck of dust
never leaks regrets, starlight, kitchen steam
never leaks quarreling neighbors, old newspapers, random junk.

Each dawn is an exception.
Then there's another. Dusk.

—translated by 鲍勃·帕里曼译 Bob Perelman

原诗 Original Poem

with wu, for hilal, by holland

a rule of staggered missives, and committed to
the non-exclusion of birds, our model for
remote intimacy and ritual is missal. this.our
near miss, our dis.tant feel
communicable.mys.tery be folded
in the arms of our best regards,

      throw
our beautifully imagined children, nearly miss
each other. since we meant each other.cornered
each other off square.cube, failed plaza, come
circle inside

sound tree.
   in every shade of green ain't nothing
going on. welcome overhear, overshare,
overcome parliament, as
intercontinental birds

直译 Literal Translation

与吴合作，为希拉尔而作，由荷兰撰作

交错的/一来一去的书信的一条规则，并致力于
鸟类不被排除，我们
远程亲密和仪式的模型/模式是弥撒用书/祈祷书 [1]·这一点·我们的
几乎错过，我们遥·远的感觉

115

可以传播的/交流的·神·秘折叠
在我们最诚挚问候的臂膀间，

        扔出
我们完美/绝美地想象出来的孩子，几乎错过
彼此 因为我们意在互相　逼着
彼此下 / 到正.方体，失败广场，来
里面转圈 / 盘旋在里面

声音的树。
        在每一款绿里没有什么
动静。欢迎无意听到，过度分享，
克服议会[2]，作为 / 如
洲际鸟[3]

译注 Notes & Explanations

1. 诗人在诗歌中使用一些同音异义词，对声音进行实验和游戏：
    missive, missal and miss.
2. "无意听到，过度分享，克服了议会"的英文原文是"overhear,
    overshare, overcome"，用了同样的"over"作为前缀，不仅押韵，而
    且引起读者对这三个词放在一起的各种思考和联想。
3. 这里的洲际鸟和前面的议会使人联想到《鸟儿大会》(The
    Conference of the Birds)。该诗为波斯诗人法里德·阿尔-丁·阿塔尔
    （Farid od-Din Attar，约 1142—约 1220）所作，共 4500 行。讲述的
    事一群鸟在带头的鸟 Hoopoe 的带领下去寻找圣地 Simorgh 的故
    事。

诗译 Poetic Translations

致及其

交错，书信往来的条文是羽灵，起到翅膀作用途
中，我们乞讨了祈祷书。这一页几乎翻过：遥遥
欲坠可以雁过拔毛。神秘合拢

我们齐道问候的胳膊，
　　　　露出孩子完美通过想象，几乎翻
过彼此，我们苦逼对方下到方正广场
在其中兜圈

音树。
　　　　每一款绿里没有气泡。无端意会，无量易
会，无复议会，如
鸟儿问答。

—translated by Che Qianzi 车前子译

在荷兰，为了希拉尔，与吴合作

书信交错
一来一去，这样的规矩
连鸟群也坦然接受，我们
远距离地爱着，远距离地举办仪式
用尽了那些弥撒用书
用尽了祷告——我们差点
错过了这一幕。这种遥、远的感觉
是可以传播的
交流的，可以在我们问候的臂弯间
神、秘折叠

　　　　　抛出一个
我们想象出的小天使，差点让我们
错过彼此——因为我们相互在意——
逼得彼此
来到正方体的失败广场
在里面瞎转悠
还想在里面盘旋
如同声音的年轮。

　　树的每一款绿里已没有
动静。你高兴时也许能听到什么，享受到什么，
若想当一只洲际鸟
必须忘掉议会这种事

—translated by Huang Fan 黄梵译

与吴合作，为希拉尔而作，由荷兰撰作

交叉投递的书信遵循着鸟类非排斥性的规矩，我们以祈祷书作为远距离
亲密和仪式的榜样。这我们几乎错失的[1]、我们遥感到的交流的神秘，
被抱挤在
我们诚挚问候的臂膀间，
　……扔出我们美丽想象出的孩子，几乎错失
彼此，因为我们是天生的一对将彼此挤出广场
立方体，这失败的商厦，来到
声音之树里

盘旋。　……每一片绿影都并非
静止。欢迎偷听，欢迎分享，
欢迎打垮议会[2]，就像
洲际飞行的鸟雀[3]

—translated by Xi Chuan 西川译

原诗 Original Poem

00

Groove conjecture in roofless happiness, oh ooh o absence and contusion,
　　rehearse and
strain in the new colonial rubble. Sufficient for
grounding refusal in plaza, real grammar

is weed ecology, out-burning of out-building, a bloom surround a picture of
  nothing but
surrounding there she go. The essence of it is way outside—multiple scenes
  for exhausting
the pure, multiple speech of impure release send her thighs' anacomputable
  flex through
past and future. Big mama's anarecombinant anima
be impossible to dress. Nothing like
no make-up for the (more + less than) ones that been reduced to a target of
  him making
himself up, faking himself whole, pushing wholeness on the hold, still ridin'
  ol' paint, still
ridin' ol' paint, stop ridin' ol' paint, goodbye ol'
paint, I'm leaving cheyenne. We emerge
in the wide border where alton and hortense persist in simulation—mooged
  boogie oogie,
muñozed ooga booga, boombridged exformation self-stimmung itself away
  up under
all that surfacing for scratched surfaces,
the surfeitry of our raggedy-ass
circuitry, till we
all decide to improve. What's enderjet + enderjet? Enderdragon. Can't expect
  how math
go, groove. Ouzhe. Than a more its notion
send can't understand. We a message
when we.

直译 Literal Translation

哦哦

契合/最佳状态/唱片上的沟纹 猜测/想象/设想在一个没有屋顶/无家的
  幸福， 哦 哦哈哈 哦 缺席和挫伤， 排练并
累/吃力/抽紧/拉伤 [1] 在新殖民瓦砾。足够

119

可以立足/树立拒绝在广场上，真的语法

是野草/大麻生态，烧空了棚子/楼房扩建的部分， 一朵花（包）围着
　　一幅画，画的是无/空但是

包围着她的本性。它的本质在外面很远/远远在外——多种情景，（情景
　　是）展现耗尽/说完

　多种（醒浊/不雅/肮脏的/混合）的（释放/在冲动下说出的脏话[2]）的
　　（单纯/纯洁）[3]的话把她大腿的不可计算的收缩[4]送到

过去和未来。（黑）大妈的不可重组的

（灵魂/女性气质）不可能穿上衣服/装扮。最好的是/没有什么像

不化妆的多+少于那些沦为/被缩小到变成一个靶子的他，捏造

他自己，把自己假装成完整的，把（他人）的整合推到/迫使停顿，还

骑着老油漆[5]， 还

骑着老油漆，别骑着老油漆，再见

老油漆，我离开夏安。我们出现在

Alton 和 Hortense[6] 还坚持模拟/拟像的那片广阔边境——合成器的布吉

哦吉/废话/毫无意义的噪音

穆尼奥斯[7]的布吉哦吉/废话/毫无意义的噪音隆隆分崩的桥/音乐中的

桥段把自己的音准/自我应激[8]定在上面偏下一点

所有那些（浮）上来为戳穿（划破的）

的表面，我们破烂的线路

的过剩，直到我们

都决定提高/变好。Enderject+ Enderject [9]是什么？末影龙。[10]预期不了
　　数学的

方向契合/达成一致乌滋[11]比一个多于它的想法/概念

传递 / 寄无法理解。我们一条

信息当我们[12]。

译注 Notes & Explanations

1. 动词
2. 和性有关
3. 诗人运用一些矛盾的修辞来表达一种复杂性。
4. 依然指代性爱
5. "Ol' Paint" 是美国民谣中的一匹马的名字

6. 雷鬼音乐乐手奥尔顿 • 埃利斯和霍尔 • 坦斯
7. 诗人的一个朋友
8. 是一个双关语。诗人将 "self-stimming" 和 "self-stimmung" 合并在一起. "Stimmung" 是德国当代作曲家施托克豪森 (Stockhausen) 为六位歌手而作的乐曲，译为《音准》。这个词的发音很像 stimulate。Self-stimming 是一个描述自闭症患者的术语，意思是 "应激性重复行为"，比如转圈、拍手、哼哼等。这种行为是为了平息大脑的混乱信号，是自我治疗的一种机制。这里诗人是在展示两个词可以听上去像是一个词，而意义是不同的。
9. 是诗人根据后面的 "Enderdragon" 的读音和前缀臆造的词。
10. "末影龙" 是电游《我的世界》中的 Boss 生物。
11. 诗人将这个名词用作象声词来表示黏糊糊、软塌塌的东西的声音
12. 最后三行的句法是非常规句法。对"and"音节的押韵。大致意思是：交流的意义不只是传递信息和理解，我们交流的时候，我们就成为信息本身。

诗译 Poetic Translation

喔喔

契合唱片上的下水道，猜测没有屋顶的家，喔喔，缺席，哈哈，挫伤，
磋商
疲倦挖犁在新殖民瓦砾。足够立足，树——立——立足在拒绝
广场，野草真的是语法，烧光棚子。扩建的楼房像花包围一幅
画，画面空洞她的本性在洞中，它的本质在远方她的大腿被脏
话乱伦又单纯地搬来运去，缠着未来与过去。大妈不可重组的
灵魂，大妈不可穿戴的气质，最好在她身边捏造如马鞍，缩小
在她身上 "吁" ，"吁" ，骑着老马还骑着老马，别骑它身
上，再见我要离开了，夏安，我们出现在
语言坚持拟声的那片广阔的废话边境，喔喔，哈哈，哼哼，哼哈，哼哈
二将

"摸你凹时!"马鞍仿佛马背上的桥,意义自闭,刺激在胸脯下
面所有浮上来的腹部,都有一个戳穿腹部的肚脐眼破烂的几条大
腿
过剩,直到都决定提高膝盖,吸钙,戏改——李小龙他预期不了药力
搬来运去寄走一条方向耷拉的龙须一条龙服务(给大妈不可穿戴的气
质配套)
我们就是龙须面

—translated by Che Qianzi 车前子译

哦哦

是唱片上最好的沟纹,让人想象一种没有家的、没有屋顶的幸福,哦
哦哈哈
哦　　是谁缺席谁挫伤,如同
在新殖民的瓦砾上排练和拉伤。这种幸福
足以让人立正,让人拒绝去广场,野草
是到处蔓延的语法,它像火焰烧空了棚子,让一朵花缠住一幅画,画
　　中充满禅意的空,但是
花已缠住她的心。而它的心已飘远——种种景象,道尽了
各种龌龊的解放的纯洁的脏话
把她大腿的伸伸缩缩献给
过去和未来。黑肤大妈一如既往的
心灵再也套不上新衣裳。真正妙的是
不化妆,比成为靶子的他俊点又丑点,他捏造
自己,把自己打扮成完人,逼别人停下,还骑着老
油漆,还
骑着老油漆,别骑着老油漆了,再见吧
老油漆,我告别了夏安。我们出现在
雷鬼音乐家执意模拟的音乐边境——合成器合成的废话
诗人朋友那隆隆欲坠的废话之桥,暗暗把自己的音调定在
河床之上,飘到

所有浮上来戳穿假象的
水面，被声音踩烂的线路
已绰绰有余，除非
我们提高嗓门真正变好。电子游戏是什么？无法预期的数学
默契，哎哟，连多于一的想法
都无法传递。当我们是一时
我们就成了消息。

—translated by Huang Fan 黄梵译

哦 哦

在无遮无拦的幸福里做老套的猜想，哦喔呃缺席和挫伤，排练并
拉拽在新殖民的瓦砾堆中。足够
在商厦里树起拒绝，真的语法
是野草生态，烧毁扩张的建筑，一朵花，包围着空白这幅画，但也是
包围着就这样的她。其本质不在其中——而在耗尽纯洁的多个现场，是
不洁的释放多次进出色语让她的大腿算计不过来地一缩一缩穿越过去和
未来。姑奶奶胡乱重组的
灵躯穿不上衣裳。啥都不像
那些简省成他的靶子的或多加或少的素颜者，这靶子让他
勃起，彻底篡改他，而他还要把握一切，还骑着名叫"老油彩"的马，
还
骑着"老油彩"，然后不骑了，再见
"老油彩"，我正要离开印第安夏安人。我们出现在
广阔的边界，这里乐手奥尔顿和霍顿斯坚持互拟——合成器的布吉哦吉
老朋友穆尼奥斯的布嘎哦嘎，在那为被戳破而表层的表层、我们腻烦的
烂腚电路图之下，将现成的
自闭疗伤的自我音准轰隆隆转化为
未知之物，直到我们
都决定变好。什么是终结喷射加终结喷射？终结龙。没法预期数学

123

怎么算，沟沟。欧了。又多冒了个想法
传出来，没法理解。我们就是
信息当我们。

—*translated by Xi Chuan 西川译*

原诗 Original Poem

previous include

I think in little involuntary trios which lets me further know, boogie, that I ain't
got no job. I ain't studying no job but I know how I'mon' live—spread out in angry

joy that three go into a buncha ways. I'm just am from I'm nowhere, everywhere
too, and culminate in further dispersal out of where 'cause I'm the bursar, baby,

and look how my sun renew
in our generate spaceship we

prepare for one another in delicacy, in window appliqué and triplicate pli and
flew catalogue, flewellyn, flung, deliciously slung, see that mouthfeel in my hand?

I just want to go thy ways! go 'head, paris, go, go on now; go on and on and on till
you gone, man, turned into every earthly elemental ornament in every, tennessee.

直译 Literal Translation

以前所包括

我用非自愿/下意识的/不由自主的小三重奏方式思考，这使我进一步了
　　解，布吉摇摆[1]，我没

工作。我不学习工作，但我知道我将这么生活——展开在愤怒的

欢乐中，（愤怒的欢乐为）三个变成一大堆方式。我来自我在无处，也
　　无处

不在，而最终/高潮达到哪里的进一步/继续扩散之处因为我是总务长 /
　　学校财务管理员，宝贝，

来看看我的太阳如何获得新生。
在我们的产生/生成飞船[2]我们

为彼此精心地准备，在窗口贴花和三重/层[3]和
飞飞目录单里[4]，弗勒艾琳[5]，扔，美美地悬挂的，看到我手里的口感
　　吗？

我只想走你的路！走吧，巴黎，走，快走；继续继续继续走直到
你已走开/你不见了，哇噢，变成每一个尘世元素点缀在每一个,田纳西。

译注 Notes & Explanations
1. 布吉是一种节奏快速的爵士钢琴舞曲，或者是快速流行乐或摇滚乐
   舞蹈。
2. Generate 原本是动词，这里变成名词。
3. 这里的 "pli" 有可能是故意的拼写错误，应该是 "ply"。"three-ply"
   和 "triplicate" 的意思类似，都是三重的意思。而 "triplicate pli" 则有
   对声音和意义进行游戏的意味。
4. "Pli and flew catalogue" 有意模仿 Ogden Nash 的一首诗
   "A Flea and a Fly in a Flue"
   A flea and a fly in a flue
   Were imprisoned, so what could they do?
   Said the fly, "let us flee!"

"Let us fly!" said the flea.
So they flew through a flaw in the flue.

　苍蝇和跳蚤被堵在烟道
　他们又能做什么呢?
　苍蝇说，"我们逃跑吧!"
"我们飞走吧!"跳蚤说，
　他们通过烟道的裂缝飞出去了

这里诗人的意思可能是批判当代消费文化对于人们的桎梏和囚禁。
"Flew Catalogue"有多重的含义，可能是"Fly"飞飞购物的商品目
录，也可以指代寡头政治下社会生活的过度严苛的秩序。

5.　据诗人本人讲，他在写下"弗勒艾琳"这个词的时候心里想的是莎
　　士比亚戏剧《亨利五世》中的人物鲁艾林（Fluellen）。他擅自在拼
　　写上做了一些改动，因为他更喜欢这个拼写看上去的样子。他说，
　　反正伊丽莎白时代的拼写也是流动的。诗人在对拼写进行一种游
　　戏。

诗译 Poetic Translations

以前所包括

下意识小三......不由自主用小三重奏思靠，这使我进一步思尻，不及摇
摆，我没立场，我不学习表态，但我知道我将怎么把我的愤怒华彩在

欢乐中，三位一体变成双飞乐章。我来自无，所以无处
不在，而最终高潮达到无处——无处女，继续扩散之处，我是奸狱长，
宝贝

来看看吾日如何获得新生
我们飞船——飞传我们

为彼此精心准备，贴窗花，开三重门，
飞吻报价表，亨利五世和盈利一世，扔掉老大，悬挂老二，看到我手里
的口交吗?

我只想走你的路！走吧，巴黎，走，快走；继续继续继续走直到
你北京，哇塞,变成每一粒尘世元素点缀"毛泽东"号和"田纳西"。

—*translated by Che Qianzi 车前子译*

从前的意味

我用被迫、无知、冲动三种方式思考，这让我洞悉了布吉摇摆，我其实
　　什么
也没做。我不学习，不工作，将生活——在愤怒的快乐中展开
愤怒的快乐是把三种思考变成一大摊浆糊。我来自我没出生的地方，也
　　无处
不在，而高潮能扩散到哪里，取决我是总务长，是校财务管理员，还是
　　宝贝？

来看看我头顶的太阳如何获得新生
它其实是我们制造的飞船，我们

为对方精心准备，在窗口贴上三层贴花
从邮寄的购物单里，掉出来鲁艾林，落到我手上，想叫我口馋吗？

我想重复你走过的路！走吧，去巴黎，快走呀；继继续续一直走到
你走开，不见了，哇噢，变成尘埃，点缀着你我心中的田纳西

—*translated by Huang Fan 黄梵译*

先前包括

我用非自愿的小三重奏方式思考，这使我，扭摆一下，更进一步知道，
我没
工作。我不费神没工作，但我知道我将这么生活——在愤怒的欢快中

展开，让三生万种方式。我是无处我就来自无处，也是无处
不在，在嗨翻之后扩散开来，因为我管钱，宝贝，

来看看我的太阳如何新生。
在我们的大力飞船里我们

为彼此精心准备，为了窗口呈现，为了使飞爽的目录册子
厚上三倍，弗勒艾琳，恣啊，美美地恣啊，看到我手里的口感吗？

我只想走你的路！走吧，巴黎，走，快走；继续继续继续走直到你
走没影，伙计，变成每一个尘世元素点缀在每一个，田纳西。

—translated by Xi Chuan 西川译

Na Ye / 娜夜

原诗 Original Poem

合影

不是你！是你身体里消失的少年在搂着我
是他白衬衫下那颗骄傲而纯洁的心
写在日记里的爱情
掉在图书馆阶梯上的书

在搂着我！是波罗的海弥漫的蔚蓝和波涛
被雨淋湿的落日　　　无顶教堂
隐秘的钟声

和祈祷……是我日渐衰竭的想象力所能企及的
那些美好事物的神圣之光

当我叹息　　甚至是你身体里拒绝来到这个世界的婴儿
他的哭声
——对生和死的双重蔑视
在搂着我

——这里　这叫做人世间的地方
孤独的人类
相互买卖
彼此忏悔
肉体的亲密并未使他们的精神相爱
这就是你写诗的理由？
一切艺术的源头……仿佛时间恢复了它的记忆
我看见我闭上的眼睛里

有一滴大海
在流淌

是它的波澜在搂着我！ 不是你
我拒绝的是这个时代
不是你和我

"无论我们谁先离开这个世界
对方都要写一首悼亡诗"

听我说：我来到这个世界就是为了向自己道歉的！

直译 Literal Translation

Group Photo

It isn't you! It's your body's faded/disappeared youngster embracing me
It's that arrogant yet pure heart beneath his white shirt
The love written in the diary
The book dropped on the library's steps

Embrace me again! It's the azure/sky blue and waves that fill the Baltic Sea
The rain-soaked setting sun   the church missing a steeple
The secret clock sound/voice

And prayer…it's what my day by day exhausted imagination can strive for
The holy light of those beautiful things

When I sigh   it's even the baby your body's insides
Won't let come into this world
His weeping
———-A twofold contempt for life and death
Is hugging me

Here   this place called the secular world
Lonely humanity
Doing business with each other
Confessing to one another
Physical intimacy hasn't made their spirits fall in love with each other

This is your reason for writing poetry? All art's
Source….as if time recovered its memory
I see in my closed eyes
There's an ocean
Flowing

It's its waves hugging me! Not you
What I reject is this era
Not you and I

"No matter which of us leaves this world first
The others all want to write an elegy"

Listen to me: I've come to this world just to apologize to myself!

诗译 Poetic Translations

Group Photo

It's not you! It's your youth embracing me, his arrogant, pure heart
beneath a white shirt, the word "love" in a diary dropped on the library
steps.

Touch me again! Here are azure waves on the Baltic sea, a soggy setting
sun, a church missing its steeple—and prayer.

All my tired imagination can still strive for:
the holy light of things.

When I sigh, it's the baby you didn't want coming into the world.
His pure contempt for life and death clings onto me

In the lonely world, people are shopping, gossiping. Not even
fucking can make their souls align.

So why do we still write poetry? What's the point? Behind my eyes, time's
flood rises. Its waves are holding me—not you.

Don't think I reject you!
"No matter which one of us leaves the world first the other shall write an
elegy."

Listen to me. I was born to apologize to myself.

—*translated by* 雷伊 艾尔曼特罗特译 *Rae Armantrout*

Group Photo

Na Ye's "Group Photo"
is a poem which despite
its title is mostly about
the lyric speaker and
a very carefully obscured
second person addressee
which may or may not
actually be the speaker
themself. There are
wild exclamatory passages
followed by ellipses
which are the silent equivalent
of the exclamation if you
recall that real exclamation
"ex-clamates" that is
shouts-out or out-shouts
in a space and takes total

tyrannical control just as
the ellipsis makes a
shadow in the moving
syntax of a poem. My
favorite moment is when
it asks "This is your
reason for writing poetry?"
after a reflection that for
the poet at least and
for their addressee, if it
is in fact somebody else,
fucking hasn't brought
about the love so deep
you end up writing elegiacal
lyric verse about it, it ends
with an apology that I
barely believe but love all
the more for my incredulity.

—*translated by* 布兰登 布朗译 *Brandon Brown*

Pair Selfie
                    (after Na Ye's "Group Photo")

Not you but your unborn twin
embraces me, naively arrogant
in a ruffled poet shirt
writing dumb love poems
in abandoned notebooks…

Oh! Baisez-moi encore!
I'm mazurka-blue in a banausic sea.
Pain's soaking everyone.
I'm missing people.
The secret clock is…operatic.

My imagination's exhausted
by the phony light
of beautiful things.

My heavy sigh's a foetus
that will be curettage,
its annoying wail contemptuous
of life and death equally.

It hugs me here in this "secular world"
where Eleanor Rigby does business
with Bartleby. They tell each other secrets
and even fuck, but never fall in love
"spiritually."

Oy vey! *This* is your reason for writing poetry?
All art's a sauce
and rhyme's recovered its threnody.
I see in my closed eyes
a boiling ocean

and I'm fucked by waves—not by you—
so I reject the contemporary—
not its pronouns—

Let us pledge to write
each other's elegies.

Listen [to self]!

      I'm sorry
              I'm so sorry
      I'm sorry

—translated by 娜达 高登译 *Nada Gordon*

原诗 Original Poem

喜悦

这古老的火焰多么值得信赖
这些有根带泥的土豆　　白菜
这馒头上的热气
萝卜上的霜

在它们中间　　　我不再是自己的
陌生人　　　生活也不在别处

我体验着佛经上说的：喜悦

围裙上的向日葵爱情般扭转着我的身体：
老太阳　　　你好吗？

像农耕时代一样好？
一缕炊烟的伤感涌出了谁的眼眶

老太阳　　我不爱一个猛烈加速的时代
这些与世界接轨的房间……

朝露与汗水与呼啸山风的回声——我爱
一间农耕气息的厨房　　和它
黄昏时的空酒瓶

小板凳上的我

135

直译 Literal Translation

Bliss

How trustworthy this old flame is
These potatoes   cabbages with their roots in the mud
This steam/heat above the steamed bun
Frost on the carrot

Among them   I no longer belong to myself
Strangers   life isn't elsewhere either

I'm experiencing what the Buddhist texts speak of: joy

The love of the sunflower on the apron[1] turns halfway around my body:
Old sun   how are you?

As good as in the age/era of agriculture?
The sadness of a wisp of smoke has sprung/poured out of the rim of
    whose eye

Old sun   I don't love a fiercely accelerating age/era
These rooms that connect the world…

The morning dew and sweat and the echo of the whistling mountain wind—
    I love
A kitchen that smells like farming   and its
Dusk's empty wine bottle

The me of the little wooden stool/bench

译注 Notes & Explanations
1. "The love of the sunflower on the apron" indicates the sunflower's
   love (not love for the sunflower)

诗译 Poetic Translations

Bliss

The sunflower on the apron wraps halfway around my body
as if in love.

How are you, sun?
As good as in the "age of agriculture"?

How reliable this old flame is. And these potatoes, cabbages,
with their roots in mud.

This steam heat above a steamed bun. Frost
on a carrot.

With them, I no longer belong to myself. What a relief!
It's what the Buddhist texts speak of:
"happiness."

But there's unhappiness too—
its contrail on the horizon.
I don't love the bullet trains,
the chat rooms linking up
to *connect* the world.

I'll take the whistle of a mountain wind,
a kitchen that smells of farming,
the "I" of dusk's empty wine bottle,

this wooden stool.

—translated by 雷伊 艾尔曼特罗特译 *Rae Armantrout*

Bliss

I share with the Chinese
poet Ne Ya a true adoration
of the *mise en scene* in which
root vegetables are cooked
with steamy carbs. Not
only the scene in which they
are cooked but in which they
are devoured as I recall
with great tenderness
a meal with Jocelyn, Yosefa
and Mat in Toronto at a place
could it really have been
called "Mother's Dumplings"
yes. When I think of it I
share Ne Ya's sentiment
in their poem "Bliss" where
they write, "I'm experiencing
what the Buddhist texts speak
of: joy." Is joy as good as
agriculture? I think so. Is it
as good as the "fiercely
accelerating era" that Ya's
poem refers to with some
degree of melancholy even
for all of the love and joy
which permeates their
lines? I think it's even
better. Joy that is. The
poem ends where it
begins, in the kitchen, a
kitchen that smells like
"farming" and where even
though the wine is gone

it is okay to sit in there
on a little wooden stool.

—translated by 布兰登 布朗译 *Brandon Brown*

Bliss

How trustworthy this old mud is,
these word dews with their roots in the dusk,
the steam above the Buddhists
and strangers on the long carrot.

Among them I no longer belong to myself.
Life isn't exactly agriculture, either.

The echo on the apron turns halfway
around my body as if in a wine bottle.
Old sweat, how are you?

As good as in the era of steamed buns?
Out of the duct of whose eye
has the dry ice of a wisp of sadness poured?

Old bun, I don't love a fiercely accelerating
algebra, or these rooms that connect
the wind.

The morning wine and carrot, and the echo
of the whistling mountain cabbage I love

A kitchen that smells like sadness,
and its empty steamed sunflower…

The I of the little wooden wisp.

—translated by 娜达 • 高登译 *Nada Gordon*

原诗 Original Poem

睡前书

我舍不得睡去
我舍不得这音乐　这摇椅　这荡漾的天光
佛教的蓝
我舍不得一个理想主义者
为之倾身的：虚无
这一阵一阵的微风　　并不切实的
吹拂　　仿佛杭州
仿佛正午的阿姆斯特丹　　这一阵一阵的
恍惚
空
事实上
或者假设的：手——

第二个扣子解成需要　过来人都懂
不懂的　解不开

直译 Literal Translation

The Bedtime Book/Written before Going to Bed[1]

I am reluctant to go to sleep
I am reluctant to let go of this music　　this rocking chair　　this rippling
daylight/light from heaven/the sky
Buddhism's blue/the Buddhist blue
I am reluctant to let go of what an idealist
Has thrown/scarified his/her entire life for：nothingness/void/emptiness
This gust after gust of breeze　　not at all realistic
Caresses　　seems like/as if Hangzhou
Seems like/as if noon's Amsterdam　　this gust after gust of

Absent-mindedness/Entrancement
Emptiness
In fact/Actually
Or supposed/presumably: hand—

The second button loosens into/opens into need   an experienced person/a person who has had it before
Completely comprehending/understands/knows
The uncomprended/Those who don't know it   can't open

译注 Notes & Explanations:

1. Judging from the content of the poem, the word "书" ("shu" in Pin Yin) is believed to be a verb, meaning "written" here. If used as a noun, it would indeed mean "book".

诗译 Poetic Translations

The Bedtime Book

I don't want to sleep, don't want to let go of this music, this chair,
this rippling daylight -Buddhist blue. I hate to let go
of what a dreamer gave her whole life for: the unbelievable caresses
of the void. The blue waters of Hangzhou, of Amsterdam at noon,
wave after wave of entrancement's phantom hand.

The second button opens into need. Someone who's touched it knows it
    has no end.
Those who haven't
know nothing

—*translated by* 雷伊 艾尔曼特罗特译 *Rae Armantrout*

Poem Written Before Bed

No, seriously, Na Ye,
I get this. I never want

to go to bed it feels like
voluntarily relinquishing
light which is the actual
fibrous matter of living
and I knew this even at
eighteen years old for at that
time I was part of a loose
and hilarious organization
known as the Sleep Resistance
we called each other "comrade"
and when one of us was
nodding off another would
come by with a cup of
hot coffee and say no Vince
get up you do not want
to succumb to the bourgeois
exercise known as slumber
until you *must*. So I too have
laid there so many night
bitter and grieving, thinking
about my dumb ass
poetry, thinking about as you
write the "uncomprehended"
the ones who will never
understand how good it is
to be awake, to be alive
although to be fair my friend
in my dotage I have come
to appreciate the folds of
a pillow and the folds of
a dream and the folds of
the body curling next to me
warm and full of noise
keeping me intoned.

—*translated by* 布兰登 布朗译 *Brandon Brown*

Hypnagogic Poem
(after Na Ye's "Bedtime Book")

The Buddhist blue sky—its rippling light—
I can't detach from
in order to fall asleep

this tune
this rocking chair
and the nothingness
I can't detach from

I can't let go
I WON'T let go

People sacrifice their lives
for the sake of this billowing void

And the mind blows
and the mind blows…
not at all realistic
caresses

Suddenly Huangzhou
is Amsterdam at noon

gusts of daze
gusts of trance

–MU–

or maybe…hand?

The second button opens into need.
I've been around the block

and I completely get it:

the incomprehensible…
THOSE WHO DON'T KNOW IT

CAN'T

OPEN

—*translated by* 娜达·高登译 *Nada Gordon*

鲍勃·帕里 / **Bob Perelman**

原诗 Original Poem

Praise or Blame

I mean this says the written body a lame duck
a world without money still as a written line

I mean this says the written body a lame duck
market the results or at least publish them

a world without money still as a written line
distribution determines rank a literary word

without a past magazines printed at irregular
intervals don't remind me a constantly broken

market the results or at least publish them
distribution determines rank a literary word

intervals don't remind me a constantly broken
seque nce of investments the imperfect tense I

was moving a chair hearing a clock tower ring
without a past magazines printed at irregular

I remember buying but not reading the *Tibetan
Book of the Dead* I've parted my hair the same

place since age ten the original word without
seque nce of investments the imperfect tense I

was moving a chair hearing a clock tower ring
echo "younger than spring time" a sentimental

145

education is always one life too late so that
when the spectacle touches my body I'm slid

into the trench history's an umbrella made of
echo "younger than spring time" a sentimental

place since age ten the original word without
education is always one life too late so that

I remember buying but not reading the Tibetan
machines twenty clouds in the sky and all for

naught a problem the non-biodegradable future
will inherit with its characteristically bent

into the trench history's an umbrella made of
sense of purpose the date is grey in grey and

alive in a spread-sheet morguish way shows of
force torching the human buildings twisted

place since age ten the original word without
depth torching the human buildings twisted

seque nce of investments the imperfect tense I
dead satisfaction left never mind the feeling

intervals don't remind me a constantly broken
echo "younger than spring time" a sentimental

victory utter annihilation the body following
circular songs of praise and blame knit tight

force torching the human buildings twisted
into the trench history's an umbrella made of

victory utter annihilation the body following
like a dog children wake in chapter eleven of

the Bhopal Trilogy men from Big Blue ride the
painted wooden helicopters above the hospital

crib no need to render details unto Caesar in
our lifetimes outtakes stand for authenticity

market the results or at least publish them
a world without money still as a written line

victory utter annihilation the body following
like a dog children wake in chapter eleven of

our lifetimes outtakes stand for authenticity
the Bhopal Trilogy men from Big Blue ride the

solemn confusion around the career trajectory
only authority can be present the audience is

free to attend as attendant nutshells dance a
solemn confusion around the career trajectory

shoehorning the credit-worthy fifteen million
into cars the face and the voice copyright in

solemn confusion around the career trajectory
machines twenty clouds in the sky and all for

dead satisfaction left never mind the feeling
painted wooden helicopters above the hospital

a world without money still as a written line
alive in a spread-sheet morguish way shows of

victory utter annihilation the body following
into cars the face and the voice copyright in

a world without money still as a written line
sense of purpose the date is grey in grey and

I mean this says the written body a lame duck
shoehorning the credit-worthy fifteen million

intervals don't remind me a constantly broken
Book of the Dead I've parted my hair the same

crib no need to render details unto Caesar in
circular songs of praise and blame knit tight

直译 Literal Translation

称赞和责备

我的意思是这说明/它是说这书写/被书写的身体是一只跛足的鸭子
一个世界没有钱依然是一行笔迹

我的意思是这说明/它是说这书写/被书写的身体是一只跛足的鸭子
推销/出售这结果/成果或至少出版它们

一个世界没有钱依然是一行笔迹
发行决定等级一个文学词汇

没有一份过去的杂志被印刷在不规则的
间歇不要提醒我一种不断破碎的

推销/出售这结果/成果或至少出版它们
发行决定等级一个文学词汇

148

间歇不要提醒我一种不断破碎的
投资序列这不完全的时态我

曾移动一把椅子听见一个钟塔敲响
没有一份过去的杂志被印刷在不规则的

我记得买过但没有读过《西藏
生死书》我已分开我的头发同样的

地方自从十岁原来的词汇没有
投资序列这不完全的时态我

曾移动一把椅子听见一个钟塔敲响
回声/回映着"比春天还年轻"一种情感

教育[1]总是晚一个生命/迟一辈子到来因此
当这景象/惨状触动我的身体我被滑

入沟渠历史是一把雨伞由...做成
回声/回映着"比春天还年轻"一种情感的/感伤的

地方自从十岁原来的词汇没有
教育总是晚一个生命/迟一辈子到来因此

我记得买过但没有读过《/西藏
机器二十朵云在天空都为了

不是一个问题这生物不可降解的未来
将继承典型的弯曲的特征

进入沟渠历史是一把雨伞由...做成
目的性/目的感日子是灰色中的灰色而且

149

活在/生存在一个数据表格停尸房 [2] 一样表现
力量点燃人类大厦扭曲的

地方自从十岁原来的词汇没有
深度点燃人类大厦扭曲

投资序列这不完全的时态我
死寂的满足感剩下不在乎/不顾这感受

间隙不要提醒我一种不断破碎的
回声/回映着"比春天还年轻"一种情感的/感伤的

胜利完全消灭身体随着
赞颂和责备的循环歌曲紧密勾连

力量点燃人类大厦扭曲
进入沟渠历史是一把雨伞由...做成

胜利完全消灭身体随着
像一个狗孩子醒来在第十一章节

《博帕尔三部曲》[3] 里 IBM[4] 的人乘着这
涂漆木制的直升飞机在医院上空

婴儿床归于凯撒 [5] 在
我们的一生的剪余片/被剪片段代表真实性

出售/推销这结果或至少出版它们
一个世界没有钱依然是一行笔迹

胜利完全消灭身体随着
像一个狗孩子醒来在第十一章节

我们的一生的剪余片/被剪片段代表真实性
《博帕尔三部曲》里 IBM 的人乘着这

严肃的困惑围绕职业轨道/轨迹
只有权威能出场观众是

作为随从/侍者果壳们自由参加舞蹈
严肃的困惑围绕职业轨道/轨迹

硬塞进 [6] 信誉好的一千五百万
到车里这脸和声音的版权在

严肃的困惑围绕职业轨道/轨迹
机器二十朵云在天空都为了

死寂的满足感剩下不在乎/不顾这感受
涂漆木制的直升飞机在医院上空

一个世界没有钱依然是一行笔迹
活在/生存在一个数据表格停尸房一样表现

胜利完全消灭身体随着
到车里这脸和声音的版权在

一个世界没有钱依然是一行笔迹
目的性这日子是灰色中的灰色而且

我的意思是这说明/这是说书写/被书写的身体是一只跛足的鸭子
硬塞进信誉好的一千五百万

间歇不要提醒我一种不断地破坏
生死书》我已分开我的头发同样的

婴儿床不需要将细节给/归于凯撒
赞颂和责备的循环歌曲紧密勾连

译注 Notes & Explanations

1. 这句话的意思是我们的教育总是关于过去，而不是现在，特别是情感教育。《情感教育》(*Sentimental Education*)是法国小说家福楼拜的名著。
2. "morguish" 是一个臆造的形容词，是名词 morgue 的变形，用来修饰 "way"。
3. "Big Blue" 在口语中指代 IBM 公司。
4. 博帕尔是印度中部的一个城市。1984 年 12 月 3 日，位于该城市北郊的美国联合碳化物公司 (UCC) 印度分公司的农药厂发生严重的毒气泄漏事故。事故发生后不久，至少有 145 件诉讼在美国联邦法院提起，其中包括印度政府作为原告对美国跨国公司提起的诉讼。被告 UCC 提出了不方便法院原则拒绝诉讼的动议。译者推测这首诗歌里的"三部曲"指的是美国法院用来判断该诉讼是否符合所谓的"不方便法院原则"的三个条件。
5. 这句诗来自《圣经新约》中的一句话：让上帝的归上帝，恺撒的归恺撒。意思是各走各的路，井水不犯河水。
6. 动词 "shoehorning" 是根据名词 shoehorn (鞋拔子) 变形而来的，意思是像鞋拔子塞进鞋里那样。

诗译 Poetic Translations

称赞和责备

说这书写的肉身是一只跛老鸭一个世界没钱只是一行笔迹它是说这书写的肉身是一只跛老鸭出售这结果或至少出版它们一

个世界没钱只是一行笔迹发行决定等级一个文学词汇没有一份旧杂志被印刷在不规则的间歇不要提醒我一种不断破碎

的出售这结果或至少出版它们发行决定等级一个文学词汇间歇不要提醒我一种不断破碎的投资序列这不完全的时态我曾

移动一把椅子听见钟楼敲响没有一份旧杂志被印刷在不规则
的我记得买过但没读过《西藏生死书》我已分开我的头发同

我曾移动一把椅子听见钟楼敲响回声"比春天还年轻"一种
情感教育总是晚一个生命到来因此当这景象触动我的身体我

被滑入沟渠历史是一把雨伞由做成回声"比春天还年轻"一
种情感地方自从十岁原来的词汇没有教育总是晚一个生命到

来因此我记得买过但没有读过机器二十朵云在天空都为了不
是一个问题这不可降解的未来将继承典型的弯曲特征进入沟

渠历史是一把雨伞由做成目的性日白生是灰色中的灰色而且
活在一个数据表格停尸房一样表现力量点燃人类大厦扭曲的

地方自从十岁原来的词汇没有深度点燃人类大厦扭曲投资序
列这不完全的时态我死寂的满天还年轻"一种情感胜利完全

消灭身体随着赞颂和责备的循环歌曲紧密勾连力量点燃人类
大厦扭曲进入沟渠历史是一把雨伞由做成胜利完全消灭身体

随着像一个狗孩子醒来在第十一章节《博帕尔三部曲》3 里
IBM 的人乘着这木制的涂漆直升飞机在医院上空婴儿床归于

凯撒在我们的一生被剪片段代表真实性出售这结果或至少出
版它们一个世界没钱只是一行笔迹胜利完全消灭身体随着像

一个狗孩子醒来在第十一章节我们的一生被剪片段代表真实性《博帕尔
三部曲》里 IBM 的人乘着这严肃的困惑围绕职业

轨迹只有权威能出场观众是作为随从果壳们自由参加舞蹈严
肃的困惑围绕职业轨迹硬塞进性能好的一千五百万到车里这

脸和声音的版权在严肃的困惑围绕职业轨迹机器二十朵云在
天空都为了死寂的满足感不顾这感受木制的涂漆直升飞机在

医院上空一个世界没钱只是一行笔迹活在一个数据表格停尸
房一样表现胜利完全消灭身体随着到车里这脸和声音的版权

在一个世界没钱只是一行笔迹目的性日白生是灰色中的灰色
而且说这书写的肉身是一只跛老鸭硬塞进性能好的一千五百

万间歇不要提醒我一种不断地破坏生死书》我已分开我的头
发同样的婴儿床不需要将细节归于凯撒在赞颂和责备的循环

—translated by Che Qianzi 车前子译

赞颂与叱责

我的意思是说被书写的身体是一只瘸腿鸭子
一个一名不文的世界依然是一行笔迹

我的意思是说被书写的身体是一只瘸腿鸭子
推销这些产品或至少出版它们

一个一名不文的世界依然是一行笔迹
而发行则决定一个文学词汇的等级

没有一份过期的杂志被非法印刷
幕间休息不再提醒我那持续的破碎声

推销这些产品或至少出版它
们发行则决定一个文学词汇的等级

幕间休息不再提醒我那持续的破碎声
跻身投资的行列未完成时态的我

曾移动一把椅子听见一个钟塔敲响
没有一份过期的杂志被非法印刷

我记得买了但没有读过《西藏
生死书》我已分开我的头发同样

某地自从十岁起原来的词汇没有了
跻身于投资的行列未完成时态的我

曾移动一把椅子听见一个钟塔敲响
回荡"比春天还年轻"的伤感

教育总是迟到于当下的生命因此
当这惨状触动我的身体我被滑倒

跌入沟渠的历史是由回荡着
"比春天还古老的"的一把雨伞的伤感构成

某地自十岁起原来的词汇没有了
教育总是迟到于当下的生命因此

我记得买了但没有读《西藏一（以下插播）
机械制造的二十朵云在天空都为了

泡影一个不可降解生物的未来
将继承典型的弯曲的特征

跌入沟渠的历史是由抵达灰中之灰
那一把雨伞的目标构成

活在一个停尸房般的数据表格显示
点燃人类扭曲大厦的力量

某地自从十岁起原来的词汇就没有了
深渊点燃人类扭曲的大厦

跻身于投资的行列未完成时态的我
死寂的满足感只剩下无所谓

幕间休息不再提醒我那不断的破碎声
回荡"比春天还年轻"的伤感

成功彻底消灭了身体随着
赞颂和责备的循环之歌它们暗通款曲

力量点燃人类扭曲的大厦
跌入沟渠的历史是由成功彻底消灭

身体的一把雨伞构成
像一个狗孩醒来在第十一章节

《博帕尔三部曲》里 IBM 的人乘着
涂漆的木头直升飞机在医院上空

婴儿床归于凯撒在
我们一生真实的剪余片

推销这些产品或至少出版它们
一个一文不名的世界依然是一行笔迹

成功彻底消灭了身体随着
像一个狗孩醒来在第十一章节

我们一生真实的剪余片
《博帕尔三部曲》里 IBM 的人乘着这

严肃的困惑围绕职业轨道
只有权威能出场而观众

作为随从而果壳们自由参加舞蹈
严肃的困惑围绕职业轨道

鞋跟里塞进好信誉的一千五百万
到车里这脸和声音的版权在

严肃的困惑围绕职业轨道
机械制造的二十朵云在天空都为了

死寂的满足感只剩下无所谓
涂漆的木头直升飞机在医院上空

一个一名不文的世界依然是一行笔迹
活在一个停尸房般的数据表格显示

成功沉底消灭了身体随着
到车里这脸和声音的版权还在

一个一名不文的世界依然是一行笔迹
而且是在灰中之灰抵达目的之时

我的意思是说被书写的身体是一只瘸腿鸭子
鞋跟里塞进好信誉的一千五百万

幕间休息不再提醒我那不断的破碎声（插播结束）
生死书》我已分开我的头发同样

婴儿床不需要将细节归于凯撒当
赞颂和责备的循环歌曲它们暗通款曲

—translated by Lan Lan 蓝蓝译

称赞和责备的反反复复

我想说的是 被写出来的是瘫了的鸭子
这世界即便没有钱 还是能留下一行被写下来的线索

我想说的是 被写出来的是瘫了的鸭子
推销或卖掉或至少看着它被印成书

这世界即便没有钱 还是能留下一行被写下来的线索
怎样卖掉它 看得出文学的高下

没有一份出版了的杂志会没规矩地印出来
别提醒我那是会不断破碎的

推销或卖掉或者至少看着它被印成书
怎样卖掉这书 看得出文学的高下

别提醒我不断破碎的那些
我也不知道此刻我在哪儿

曾经去移一把椅子 而一只钟正在高塔那儿敲响
没有一份杂志会没规矩就印出来

我记得买过《西藏
生死书》但没有读它 我的头发就此分开了

从那时候 从十岁起就知道没有原本的意思
我也不知道此刻我在哪儿

曾经去移一把椅子时 一只钟它在高塔那儿敲响
回声环绕 类似 "比春天还年轻" 的情感

教育总是比人晚来一辈子 因此
这悲惨接触到了我的身体 我正滑倒

进入深沟 历史这把雨伞由什么什么做成
回声环绕 类似 "比春天还年轻"的情感

从十岁起就知道没有原本的意思
教育总是比人晚来一辈子 因此

我记得买了《西藏…而没有读
机器给天空造了二十朵云彩

不是一个问题 这生命没有可操作的未来
它将长久地把弯曲的特性留在自己身上

进入深沟 历史这把雨伞由什么什么做成
日子都有目的 在灰色中间还有灰色深藏 而且

活在数字表格里 那是它的停尸房
人类的大厦被力量扭曲着

那儿 十岁起就知道没有原本的意思
燃烧 人类的大厦扭得越来越变形

这就是不完整的我
寂静的濒死多么好 看我多不在乎

别提醒我 那不断碎掉的回响
那"比春天还年轻"的悲伤

胜利彻底销毁了我能望得见的身体 而随着
又赞美又责难的循环反复 一个曲子头尾相连

人类的大厦被力量扭曲着
进入深沟 历史这把雨伞由什么什么做成

胜利彻底销毁我能望得见的身体
像只狗一样的孩子在第十一章醒过来

《博帕尔三部曲》里 IBM 的人乘上了
涂了漆的木飞机在医院头顶上盘旋

婴儿床是凯撒的
我们的一生被剪碎 片片段段说明我们来过这世界

推销或卖掉或至少看着它被印成书
这世界即便没有钱 还是能留下一行被写下来线索

胜利彻底销毁我能望得见的身体
狗一样的蜷缩着的孩子在第十一章醒来

我们的一生被剪碎 片片段段说明我们来过这世界
《博帕尔三部曲》里 IRM 的人乘着这

一本正经的困惑环绕着的轨迹
只有权贵才能登场 而观众

只是随从 果壳们跑出来欢蹦乱跳
一本正经的困惑环绕着的轨迹

塞进早答应过的一千五百万 这硬通货
在车里面 这脸和循环的声响都是合法的

一本正经的困惑环绕着的轨迹
机器给天空造了二十朵云彩

寂静的濒死多好 看我多不在乎
涂了漆的木飞机 在医院头顶上转

这世界即便没有钱 还是能留下一行被写下来的线索
活在数字表格里 那是它的停尸房

胜利彻底销毁我能望得见的身体
在车里面 这脸和循环的声响都是合法的

这世界即便没有钱 还是能留下一行被写下来的线索
这灰色中深藏灰色 并且

我想说的是 被写出来的是一只瘸了的鸭子
硬塞进了一千五百万 这硬通货

歇一会儿 不要提醒我 不断破坏
…生死书》我的头发已经分开

婴儿床不必把细节归给凯撒
又赞美又责难 循环反复 一个曲子头尾相连

—translated by Wang Xiaoni 王小妮译

Wang Xiaoni / 王小妮

原诗 Original Poem

月光白得很

月亮在深夜照出了一切的骨头。

我呼进了青白的气息。
人间的琐碎皮毛
变成下坠的萤火虫。
城市是一具死去的骨架。

没有那个生命
配得上这样纯的夜色。
打开窗帘
天地正在眼前交接白银
月光使我忘记我是一个人。

生命的最后一幕
在一片素色里静静地彩排。
月光来到地板上
我的两只脚已经预先白了。

直译 Literal Translation

The Moon is White Indeed

The moon illuminates/exposes/shows the bones of everything at night

I breathe in the air of bluish white
The minute/trivial skin and hair of the human world
Turned into drowning/falling fireflies
This city is a dead skeleton

No life
Deserves this pure color of night
I see, right in front of me
As the curtains pulled apart
Silver is being exchanged between heaven and earth/changing hands between
    heaven and earth
The moon makes forget I am a person/human

The last act/scene of life
Is rehearsing quietly in this plainness/plain color
The moonlight steps on the floor
My feet have turned white even before it comes.

诗译 Poetic Translations

The Moon is White Indeed

At night the moon x-rays everything;

I breathe in what's left
Of our little human world,
Our floating hair and skin
reduced to scattered fire flies.
Our city's a skeleton.

No one deserves
The pure colors of night.
I stare straight ahead
As the curtains are pulled back
And heaven and earth exchange
Their silver needles.

The moon makes me forget
I'm a person.
I rehearse my last breath
On this bare stage.

—*translated by* 雷伊 艾尔曼特罗特译 *Rae Armantrout*

REALLY GREAT MOON

What if instead of the moon…
well that's a dumb thought
so instead of thinking it
I thicken whiskey with sugar cube
cut cutie, muddle, mix, sigh, go look
at the tree all lit up with spring
light, the light of the moon
in daylight. Off grass and bugs
and finally the whole city
reflecting off my head.
Soon I won't have any hair
on my head, and my eyes
and nose and mouth will
crown a kind of big moon.
Patrick Macaw slides on a
crease through three Spurs
to the rim goddamn it and
the moon is fine, the moon
is good. Wang Xiaoni knows
and the chives and the dill.
The moon is fine and good
but gives no fucks for me
or for Patrick Macaw
or the slender whizzing tree.
It's altogether a kind of
moondance. I'm not talking
about anything Van Morrison.
This poem is about the moon.

—*translated by* 布兰登 布朗译 *Brandon Brown*

The Moon is White Indeed

Tonight the moon shines through to the bones.

And so I breathe the blue air.
The trivial skin of the human world

Evanesces into fireflies.
The city is a skeleton.

No life is good enough for this transparent no-color
That's right in font of me.
As the curtains part
On the silvery communication between earth and sky
The moon makes me forget I'm alive.

Life's last act
Rehearses in whispers.
As the moonlight touches the floor
My feet are transparent.

—*translated by* 鲍勃·帕里曼译 *Bob Perelman*

原诗 Original Poem

寻仇者

那凌空的一条
吓人一跳。
镖客，打铁的，吹玻璃的都缩到暗处
只剩了那条锋利
高悬，凉的，炯炯有世仇
定一定神，瞄着这黑的人间。

眼看要趁着风力斜旋下落
它的对手急了
要扑向阴影里去避难。
一棵老透了的金桂
满头翘着浮起的碎花。
寻仇的就要刺过这温吞迷醉的树
看那月光，箭似的下旋。

直译 Literal Translation

The Avenger

That hop/jump in the air
Shocks/Scares people
The armed escorts/body guards, the blacksmith, the glassware makers/the
glass blowers all tucked/huddled in the dark
Only that slim/thin piece of sharpness
Hang in the air, cold, shining with fiery resentment
It pulls itself together, aiming at this black/dark world

It prepares itself for/will soon start the journey of spinning down in the wind
Its rival/competitor becomes anxious/heated
Who plunges into the darkness and seeks refuge there
A real old/mature sweet olive with
Tiny flowers floating on its head
The avenger will stab through this gentle and intoxicating tree
And then watch the moon fall like swirling arrows.

诗译 Poetic Translations

The Avenger

It's that leap into thin air
That scares people:
Body guards, armed escorts, a blacksmith
All cower in the dark.
Only that sickle is visible, bright
With resentment. It pulls itself together
And aims at this murky world.

But it too should prepare itself.
It will be made redundant.
Its hot headed rival will plunge into darkness
To coat its rage in olive oil.
Then its vengeance will slip through

Even this gentle grove.
And the moon will waste its last arrows.

—translated by 雷伊 艾尔曼特罗特译 *Rae Armantrout*

REVENGE

I would never stab a tree.
Would you, Wang Xiaoni?
I guess I have stabbed a tree
but I was a young fuck
there's no way I would want
to hear it breathing, gasping
those last leaves of breath
swish, dagger in the net.
Wang Xiaoni, sometimes I read
your poems as tranquil
strong sativa by the beach. They
sort of make the world feel
less scary but it is not less
scary. At my worst moments
I want revenge on it. The
world I mean, the whole fucking
world. The ocean and trees.
Revenge not for myself but
for olives and little flowers.
Who would stab a tree? Who
would cut the throat of a ruby?
It's on those people especially
I dearly want desperately
tearfully want revenge
an assassin from behind the arc
an armed poet in the cellar
bumping into shit. Making noise.

—translated by 布兰登 布朗译 *Brandon Brown*

The Avenger

That pulse in the air
Shocks everyone.
The body guards, blacksmiths, glass blowers
All of them huddled in the dark alleys
Away from that thin thing hanging up there, cold, fiery, resentful,
Gathering for its full shot into the dark corners.

And now it starts coming down
Which makes the competition
Plunge into the dark for shelter.
The old flowering olive with the tiny blossoms
The avenger will smash through this soft intoxication
And then watch as the moon falls to pieces.

—*translated by 鲍勃·帕里曼译 Bob Perelman*

原诗 Original Poem

自杀的鱼

月光松沓沓。
一条鱼猛一用劲跳出水池
哼了几声不动了。
四周发灰哦松沓沓。

想去摘朵新开的白兰
那香味笔直笔直
想了一年了。
直奔着花，跑过月亮地
不小心踩上这条自杀的鱼
软到吓人。

有肉的桑叶
白刺在起棱

168

小眼珠里一汪光。
赶紧后退，全忘了世上有花香
鱼哦鱼，我好无助。

直译 Literal Translation

The Fish Who Killed Itself

The moonlight shines loosely
A fish forcibly flings itself out of the pond
Groaned for a little while and then stopped
All around it, everything gives away to color grey/everything turns grey, oh,
everything is loose

I want to pluck the young white orchid/iris
The scent is steep
Have been thinking about/coveting it for a year
Running straight to the flower, passing the moon field
Stumbled into/Accidently stepped on this dead fish, soft and scary

The mulberry leaves with flesh
The white bones are ribbed and sharp
The little beady eyes shine and sparkle/shine like a pool of light
I withdrew my feet in a haste, forgetting about all the/fragrance/flowers in the
    world
Fish, oh fish. I am so helpless.

诗译 Poetic Translations

The Fish Who Killed Itself

The moonlight's hit or miss.
A fish throws itself out of its pond,
Pants for a minute, then stops.
All around it, things are giving up on color.
Everything's approximate.

I want to pluck the white orchid
Whose scent is so sharp
I've been thinking about it all year,
But instead fall on this dead fish,
Cold and slick as mulberry leaves.
I'm ready to give up on flowers.
Oh, fish, I'm so clueless.

—translated by 雷伊 艾尔曼特罗特译 *Rae Armantrout*

SUICIDAL FISH

After I tried to become a fish
Steve said don't do that
do it when you're forty
if you still want to do it
now I am almost 40 I don't
want to become a fish
or go anywhere near that
gory pond, big gasping
gills laying in the grass by it
I want to give flowers to
a fish. I want to break
free my rusty cage and run.
What do you think Wang Xiaoni?
What if you want to skip on
a moonfield, and end up
tripping on a dead fish
water on Mars?
garden of streams
I planted a mulberry
I carried a watermelon
bore into it and made a mess
ripping up a barbecue until
the bay was in me. I was
a fish or fishy. I was the
bridge, or bridgey. Chris
Cornell come back to life
and sing that one in our

ears, louder than love
I want to break free my
rusty cage and run, you
fucking fish! Come back
to life and live, I wish.

—translated by 布兰登 布朗译 Brandon Brown

Fish Suicide

The moon shines chaotically
And a fish flings itself up out of the pond,
Gasps briefly then stops.
Around it, total greyness:
Grey chaos.

I'd wanted to pluck the sweet young iris
With the sharp scent.
I'd been waiting all year
And as I pushed forward
I stepped right on this dead fish,

Like some fat mulberry leaf,
The white bones sharp,
The little eyes still sparkling.
I jumped back, forgetting the iris.
Uff -- the fish. I'm washed up too.

—translated by 鲍勃·帕里曼译 Bob Perelman

Xi Chuan / 西川

原诗 Original Poem

西川选自《出行日记》

撞死在挡风玻璃上的蝴蝶

我把车子开上高速公路，就是开始了一场对蝴蝶的屠杀；或者蝴蝶看到我高速驶来，就决定发动一场自杀飞行。它们撞死在挡风玻璃上。它们偏偏撞死在我的挡风玻璃上。一只只死去，变成水滴，变成雨刷刮不去的黄色斑迹。我只好停车，一半为了哀悼，一半为了拖延欠债还钱的时刻。但立刻来了警察，查验我的证件，向我开出罚单，命令我立刻上路，不得在高速公路上停车。立刻便有更多的蝴蝶撞死在我的挡风玻璃上。

逆行

忽然就只剩下我一辆车了。忽然就望见天上落下羊群了。忽然迎面而来的羊一只只全变成了车辆。忽然双行道变成了单行道。走着走着，忽然我就逆行了！我怎么开上了这条路？那些与我同路的车辆去了哪里？我逆着所有的车辆，仿佛逆着真善美的羊群。不是我要撞死它们，而是它们要将我温柔地踩死。走着走着，忽然我就逆行了！我就听到了风声，还有大地的安静。我没撞上任何车辆，我撞上了虚无。

变幻

黑夜和小雨使我迷路。在一段停着压路机却无人施工的路面上，一个胖子跟上了我。我加快脚步。他开始威胁和谩骂。我并不焦虑我兜里不多的钱，我焦虑这城市里只有他和我。焦虑，焦急，我一阵虚弱，忽然我就变成了三个人。我们三人停步转身，已经冲到眼前的胖子完全傻眼。他回身就跑，我们拔脚就追。我们边跑边体验人多势众的感觉真好。直到我们一起掉下一道水沟，直到我找不到我那同伴二人。

这座城市避开了我

这座城市避开了我。它给我大雨，使我不能在街头闲逛。我听说过的博物馆，因人手不够而闭馆。商店里，人们说着我听不懂的话。商店里只卖一种酒，是我不能喝的那一种。我饥肠辘辘找到的，是关了门的餐厅。

我大声抱怨，但没人在乎。我敲沿街的门，门开了，但屋里却没有人。我靠到一棵树上，树叶便落了下来。在这座城市里我没有一个熟人。哎，我到了这座城市，等于没有到过。

直译 Literal Translation

from **Travel Diary**

Butterflies smashed dead on the windshield

I drove the car onto the highway, which was precisely to begin a massacre of butterflies; or the butterflies seeing my speeding toward them, just decided to launch a suicide flight. They smashed to death on the windshield. They stubbornly mashed to death on my windshield. They died one by one, becoming water drops, becoming yellow marks the wipers can't scrape off. I could only stop the car, half to grieve their deaths, half to put off paying off debts. But at once a policeman came, checked my identification and gave me a ticket, demanding that I immediately get onto the road, and not to park on the highway. Immediately, there were more butterflies that smashed to death on my windshield.

Going the wrong way

Suddenly there remained only my car. Suddenly I spotted a flock of sheep falling from the sky. Suddenly the sheep coming head-on changed into cars one by one. Suddenly the two-way road became a one-way road. Going along, suddenly I was going the wrong way! How did I drive onto this road? Where did all the cars going the same way as I go? I went against all the cars, as if against the sheep flocks of good, truth and beauty. It is not that I wanted to smash them to death, but rather that they wished to trample me dead gently. Going along, suddenly I was going the wrong way! I only heard the

173

sound of the wind, as well as the earth's quiet/serenity. I did not hit any cars, I hit nothingness.

Fluctuation

The black night and a light rain made me lost. On a section of road where a road-roller was parked but no construction was occurring, a fat man caught up to me. I sped up my footsteps. He began to threaten me and hurl abuse. I didn't at all worry about the little money in my bag, I worried that in this city there was only him and me. Worried, anxious, in a burst of weakness, I suddenly turned into three people. The three of us stopped and turned, the fat man who had already rushed in front was completely dumbfounded. He turned around and ran, we lifted our legs and gave chase. As we ran we experienced how very good it was to be many people with the power of a crowd, until we fell together into a ditch, up until I couldn't find my two companions.

This city has evaded me

This city has evaded me. It gave me heavy rain, making me unable to idly stroll the streets. The museum I've heard of, closed due to inadequate staffing. In the store, people spoke a language I couldn't understand. The store only sold one kind of liquor, the kind I couldn't drink. What I found with stomach rumbling, was a restaurant that was closed. I loudly complained, but no one cared. I knocked on the door along the street, the door opened, but there was no one inside. I leaned against a tree, and the leaves started to fall. In this city I have not one acquaintance. Alas, coming to this city is the same as not having come at all.

诗译 Poetic Translations

from **Travel Diary**

Butterflies Smash on the Windshield

I drive my car onto the freeway, precisely when the massacre begins. Or butterflies, seeing me speed toward them, decide just then on mass suicide, smashing themselves on my windshield. Stubbornly mashing to death, one by one, becoming droplets, yellow stains my wipers can't clean away. I can only stop the car, both to grieve and to postpone paying reparations. Immediately, a policeman arrives, checks my ID and writes a ticket, ordering me along, no stopping on the freeway. Immediately, more butterflies smash to death on my windshield.

Going the Wrong Way

Suddenly, I'm the only car on the road. Suddenly, I notice a flock of sheep falling from the sky. Suddenly, the sheep come at me head-on, changing into cars, one by one. Suddenly, the road becomes one-way. I drive on. Suddenly, I'm going the wrong way! How did I get here? Where are the cars going my way? I drive against the traffic as against flocks of goodness, truth and beauty. I don't want to smash them, but rather, they want to trample me dead. Driving on, suddenly, I'm going the wrong way! But, I hear only wind and earth's serenity. I hit no cars at all. I hit nothingness.

Fluctuation

In gentle rain on a dark night, I get lost. A fat man catches up with me by a steamroller parked on the road, though there's no construction in sight. I walk faster. He begins to threaten and insult me. I'm not worried about the little bit of money in my bag. I'm worried that in this city there are only two of us, him and me. So worried and tense, in a burst of weakness, suddenly I divide into three people. All three of us stop and turn. The fat man's speed carries him past of us, dumbfounded. He runs. We hotfoot it after him. Running, we feel good to be many, with the power of a crowd, until we all fall together in a ditch, and I can't find my two companions.

This City Has Evades Me

This city evades me. Rain pours down on me. I can't idly stroll its streets. The museum I heard about is closed, due to budget cuts. In the store, people speak a language I don't know. The store sells only one kind of liquor, which I can't drink. My stomach rumbles. I find a restaurant. It's closed. I complain vehemently, but no one cares. I knock on the door, the door opens, but no one's there. I lean against a tree. Leaves fall on me. In this city, I don't know anyone. Arriving at this city is the same as never visiting it, alas.

—*translated by 白萱华译 Mei-mei Berssenbrugge*

from **Travel Diary**

Dead Butterflies

Wanted to massacre some fucking butterflies so drove my fucking car onto
the fucking highway to massacre them. They were kamikaze butterflies, they
were going to fucking kill themselves on my windshield. Splat. Fuck those
fucking butterflies, stubborn assholes all up on my windshield. One by one
they turned into drops of yellow goop. My fucking windshield wipers just
smeared them around. I stopped my rusted wreck jalopy half to mourn
them—poor little creeps—half to put off paying a huge fucking mountain of
debts. But then, fuck, a fucking COP showed up and checked my fucking ID
for fuck's sake, and demanded that I get back on the road and not park on the
goddamn highway. Immediately more of those asshole creepy-ass butterflies
smashed to death all up on my windshield.

The Wrong Fucking Way

Now there was just my car on the highway. Suddenly a huge flock of
enormous smelly sheep was falling from the sky. The highway turned into
fucking one-way street and those big fat fucking filthy sheep were charging
head on into cars one by one. Then, fuck –suddenly! –I was going the wrong
way! How the fuck did I even get here? What happened to all the fucking
cars going the same way as me? I went against all those goddamn cars
coming at me, bang, crash, get the fuck out of my way, muthafuckas – like I
was going against those pathetic-ass sheep, those flocks of "good truth" and
"beauty." Actually I didn't want to smash *them* to death, but – you know – I
wanted them to gently, gently, bit by bit, devil-spawned cloven hoof by
cloven hoof, to trample *me* to death. No luck. Suddenly I was going the other
way in total silence. I only hit the breeze sound and the earth's numbing
serenity. I didn't hit any cars. I hit nothingness.

Flux

I was lost in black night and light rain (so noir! so existential!) on a stretch of
road where a big-ass fucking road roller was parked, though there was no
construction. Suddenly an obese, slobbery dude caught up to me. "Hey
fucker you better watch your fuckin' ass, you moron loser creepy assclown
fuck," he yelled. I didn't think he was going to steal my shit, but fuck there
was me and him in this nowhere land. Luckily I split into three people. We
stopped and turned, and this nasty bunghole dude looked completely lost like

his big floppy ass-face was gonna melt. He turned and tried to run on his saggy-ass elephant legs. We, lightened into three, gave fleet and fearsome chase. Running, we reveled in our swift, willowy motion and powerful crowd-feeling until we fell down together in a ditch and I could no longer find my two clone-homies.

Slippery City

This city slipped away in heavy rain so I couldn't idly stroll its streets on some fancy dérive. I couldn't understand a fucking word of what anyone was saying, so you know, so much for situationism. The store had just one kind of nasty-ass hooch, no way would I drink that vile shit. My stomach growled nonstop so I went to the one restaurant there but wouldn't you know it was totally fucking closed. "Hey, open the fuck up, I'm fucking starving," I yelled, but no one gave a shit. I knocked on some door and it opened, but there was no one inside, just a big fucking empty humming void. I leaned on a tree and all the fucking dead-ass leaves fell off. Fuck this place. I don't know a soul here. Being here is like being totally nowhere.

—娜达·高登译 *Nada Gordon*

from **Travel Diary**

When the air was full

When I caught the trade wind, when the air was full, every small resistance found me trying to find them. The lens was moving. The prism was a festival of insect selflessness. Swarms fell before my ship like a movie. I tried to wash the spray off my hands, tried to feel bad, but there he was taking names like the burning air. Here I go. Here they come.

Turned around

Suddenly, in the recess, some thunder. The solo was a riot of vessels, the gulfstream packed with antagonism, and I got turned around. I didn't know what time it was. How sublime it was, too, that mathematical tremor in my core, core risen in the air all by myself. The moral law within was a militia and I drove through it like Ayrton Orkin. I'm not hard but don't rub me the right way. They got a way but I get turned around. Just hush and smooth in the relative calm.

Three two one

Black fell spray me all over the place. Them horrible little lego pieces on the floor had me where I couldn't get away from him. He was laughing at me tipping, at my brokenness in lego city. He said it's gon' be you and me, but when I get blue and frayed like that I trinitize. I turned and trinitized his big ass and he freaked. You shoulda seen this jolly motherfucker trying to book. We ran after him just so we could keep looking at him. We ran the way dancers run, we ran the way clubs feel, all the way back to rooms for rent.

This lying city

It's hard to wander this lying city. I'm drenched in labor and the underground museum is closed. Noah left to form an orchestra. Ils ont mis loosies en paquets parce qu'ils ne savent pas ce que signifie and that wine just settles. The spray's ubiquitous tease. My throat is dry. One door says restaurant, the other says supply, and the look on my face attracts no attention. I'm in that alley where they send the blown leaves. It's neither here nor there.

—translated by 布兰登 布朗译 *Fred Moten*

原诗 Original Poem

八段诗

1. 哪一朵色情的桃花

哪一朵色情的桃花曾梦见过这只多汁的桃子现在被我咬下一口
并想到这个问题在西王母的蟠桃园中？
我，齐天大圣，偷偷地进来，还得偷偷地出去。

2. 面向大海

面向大海，背向城市。
意图面向海底的城市，珊瑚和水母的城市，〔万年前的城市，
却看见了空中的城市，那里游荡着狗熊和山猫，是没有时间的城市。

3. 习惯性想象
一想到蛇，必是毒蛇，仿佛除了毒蛇没有蛇；
一想到鲨鱼，必是吃人的鲨鱼，仿佛全世界都是迪斯尼。
对那些无害的蛇和鲨鱼，作为一个成熟的男人，我要说一声"对不起"。

4.新江南
天空阴沉这是旧江南。新时代的小鸟飞在旧江南的天空。
旧江南的江面上机动渡轮半新不旧，虽新而旧，走着旧日的斜线。
对岸的楼房盖得比山岭高出一截这已是百分百的新江南。

5. 传统和鬼
有传统的地方人多鬼多，甚至人少鬼多，甚至无人而有鬼。
听一人讲话我知道他是鬼，但我不愿点破：
害怕吓着鬼自己，同时也吓着听他讲话的其他人。

6.关于原子弹的对话
同事说：我反对原子弹掉下来炸我一个人！另一位同事说：如果
原子弹哑了火，真有可能掉下来砸死你！
再一位同事说：什么境界呀你们这是？要是原子弹袭来你们先撤，我顶着！

7. 老演员
老演员演别人，一辈子活六十辈子，可以了。终于到了戏演完的时候，酸
甜苦辣还在继续。老演员演别人终于演到了自己的死。请安静一会儿，请
关灯。

8. 小演员
化了装的准备登台的小姑娘粉衣粉裤，肩膀露在风里。
她既不快乐也不悲伤，像其他小姑娘一样。
在迈步登上那古老的露天舞台之前的一瞬间　她提了提裤子。

直译 **Literal Translation**

Eight Poems

1. What Sexy Peach Blossom

What/which sexy peach blossom has seen in a dream this many-leafed peach
that now I am taking a bite of
And thought of this question in the Western Queen Mother's[1] peach orchard?
I, Great Sage the Equal of Heaven[2], came in stealthily, must also stealthily leave.

2. Facing the Sea

Facing the sea, back to the city.
Intending to face the city at the bottom of the sea, city of coral and jellyfish,
city of 50 thousand Years ago,
But seeing instead the city of air /or is it the city in the air, where bears and
bobcats wander, a city without time.

3. Habitual Imagination

Whenever thinking of snakes, must think of poisonous snakes, as if there are
no snakes but poisonous snakes.
Whenever thinking of sharks, must think of man-eating sharks, as if the
whole world was Disney.
To those not-poisonous snakes and sharks, as a mature man, I must say "sorry."

4. New Jiangnan /River-South[3]

Overcast sky is old Jiangnan. New time's small birds fly in Old Jiangnan's sky.
On old Jiangnan's river surface locomotive ferries are half-new not old, even
if new yet still old, going along diagonal lines of the old days.
On the opposite bank new buildings that are built higher than the mountains
are already one hundred percent New Jiangnan.

5. Tradition and Ghosts

In traditional places people are many and ghosts are many, or even /one could
even say people are few and ghosts are many, or even /one could even
say there aren't people but ghosts.

Listening to a person speak I know he is a ghost, but I don't wish to bluntly
point it out:
Afraid of scaring the ghost himself, and also afraid of scaring the others
listening to him.

6. Dialogue on the Atomic Bomb

A colleague says: I oppose the atomic bomb dropping down and exploding
me alone!
Another colleague says: If an atomic bomb mutes its fire[4], it really is possible
that it will fall and crush you!
Yet another colleague says: What state is this that you're in? If the atomic
bomb attacks you run first, I'll hold it!

7. Old Actor

Old actor plays someone else, his whole life lives sixty lives, enough.
Finally comes to the end of the play-acting, the sour sweet bitter spicy[5] of life
continue.
Old actor playing other people finally gets to play his own death. Please be
quiet for a while, please turn off the light.

8. Little/Young Actor

The made-up and ready for stage young girl (wears) pink shirt pink pants,
shoulder bared to the wind.
She is neither happy nor sad, like any other little girl. A moment before
stepping onto the ancient open-air stage she tugs her pants.

译注 Notes & Explanations

1. In the classic *The Journey to the West*, the "Western Queen Mother"
keeps the Peaches of Immortality in Heaven. The Peaches of Immortality
play a big role in Chinese mythology, particularly in *The Journey to the
West*. In the story, they are eaten by the main character, Sun Wukong,
also known as the Monkey King, when he is stationed as the Guardian of
the Peaches. Sun realizes that the peaches will make him immortal and
eats almost all of them. As a result, he runs into trouble because the
Queen Mother has been planning a peach banquet for the gods. Sun
shrinks himself to hide in one of the remaining peaches to avoid
detection.

2. This is the self-proclaimed title of Sun Wukong or the Monkey King.
3. "Jiangnan," literally "river-south," refers to the area immediately to the south of the lower reaches of the Yangtze River, including the southern part of the Yangtze Delta.
4. This means falls unexploded.
5. An idiom meaning "joys and sorrows."

诗译 Poetic Translations

Eight Poems

1. What Sexy Peach Blossoms

What sexy peach blossom saw in a dream this leafy peach I bite into and thought of this question in the orchard of immortality?
"I, great sage, Monkey King, heaven's equal, who entered in secret, must secretly leave."

2. Facing the Sea

Facing the sea with my back to the city.
Intending to face the city at the bottom of the sea, coral, jellyfish waving, city from 50,000 years ago,
But seeing instead a city in air, where bears and bobcats roam, a city beyond time.

3. Habits of Imagining

When I think of snakes, I think of poisonous ones, as if there were no other kind.
When I think of sharks, I think they're man-eating,
as if the whole world were Disneyland.
As a grown man, I apologize to all non-poisonous, non-aggressive snakes and sharks

4. New South River

The old Yangtze delta is an overcast sky. New time's small birds fly there.
On the old river's surface, engine powered ferries, nearly new aren't old or even new

182

are still old, as they move along diagonals of the old days. On the opposite
   shore,
new buildings higher than mountains are already 100% New Yangtze delta.

5. **Tradition and Ghosts**
In historic places there are many people and many ghosts, or one could say,
few people and many ghosts, or one could say, no people except ghosts.
Listening to a person speak, I know he's a ghost, but don't wish to rudely
   expose him.
I'm nervous about frightening the ghost, and also the other ones listening to
   him.

6. **Dialogue of the Atomic Bomb**
My colleague says, "I'm against an atom bomb dropping and exploding me
   all alone!"
Another says, "If the bomb is a dud, it could still fall and crush you!"
Another says: "What a state you're in! How worried! If you are attacked by
   an atom bomb,
just run and I'll grab it and hold it back!"

7. **Old Actor**
The old actor plays a role. He's lived sixty lives already, that's enough.
Finally, he's at the end of pretending the sweet and sour of life, as it goes on.
Always playing others, now he can finally play his own death. Please, be
quiet for a while. Please, turn off the lights.

8. **Young Actor**
A little girl in stage make-up wears a pink shirt and pants,
her shoulders bare to the breezes.
She's neither happy nor sad, like any little girl.
Just before entering the ancient open-air stage, she tugs up her pants.

—translated by 白萱华译 Mei-mei Berssenbrugge

Eight Poems

1.   **Sexy Peach Blossom**
Some sexy peach blossom
dreamed of the leafy peach

183

I'm now eating.

I'm the m-m-m-m-monkey king—so smart!
The equal of heaven!

I snuck in
and must sneak out, too.

2. Facing the Sea
The sea before me
The city behind me

Meaning to face the ancient undersea city
of jellyfish and coral,
but seeing instead a city in the air
where bears and bobcats wander…

A city outside of time.

3. Habitual Imagination
Snakes in my mind = venomous snakes (as if all snakes are venomous)

Sharks in my mind + man-eating sharks (as if the whole world were Disney)

To those non-venomous snakes
and non-man-eating sharks,
as a mature man,
I offer this most humble apology.

4. New Jiangnan/River South
New time's small birds
fly in Old Jiangnan's overcast sky.
On the river, ferries are half-new—
not old—going along the diagonal lines
of the old days.

On the opposite bank,
new buildings, higher than mountains:
100% New Jiangnan!

5. Tradition and Ghosts
In traditional places
people are many and
ghosts are many

or

People are few and
ghosts are many

or

There aren't people—
just ghosts.

Listening to one guy speak
I know he is a ghost
but don't wish to bluntly
point it out.

I'm afraid to scare the ghost himself
and afraid of scaring the others
around us.

6. Conversation on the Atomic Bomb
A: I oppose the atomic bomb dropping down and exploding me alone!
B: If an atomic bomb mutes its fire, it could possibly fall and crush you!
C: If the atomic bomb attacks you, run first! I'll hold it!

7. Old Actor
The old actor has inhabited
sixty lives. It's enough.

Finally the curtain descends
but the sour-sweet-bitter-spiciness
of his life continues.
Having played all those other people
he finally gets to play his own death.

Please be quiet for a while.

Please turn out the light.

8.   Toddler in Tiara

Lips glossed, curls tossed,
cheeks all ablush,
the same color as her outfit.

Her tiny shoulder exposed,
she is neither happy nor sad,
like any other little girl.

A moment before stepping
in front of the cameras
she tugs her pants

—*translated by* 娜达 高登译 *Nada Gordon*

Eight Poems

1.   What Sexy Peach Blossom

What sexy peach blossom
has seen in a dream this
many-leafed peach that
now I take a bite of,

and thought of this
question in the Western
Queen Mother's orchard?

I, Great Sage, the Equal
of Heaven, who came in
stealth and in stealth
must also leave.

2.   Facing the Sea
Facing the sea,
back to the city,

meaning to face
the city at the
bottom of the sea,
city of coral and
jellyfish, city of
fifty thousand
years ago,

but seeing instead
the city of air,
or the city in air,
where bears and
bobcats wander,

a city out of
time

3.   Habitual Imagination
When thinking of snakes,
I always think of
poisonous snakes, as if
there are no others.

When thinking of sharks,
I only think of
maneaters, as if Disney
were the world.

187

To the snakes that
don't poison and the
sharks that don't eat
men, as a grown man,
I have to say I'm sorry.

4. New Jiangnan

Old Jiangnan is overcast
sky. New time's small birds
run that thickness.

On the surface of old
Jiangnan's river,
locomotive ferries are
Half-new, not old, even
if new still old, gone
on, inclining
to the old days.

On the other bank, new
buildings, higher than
the mountains, already
all New Jiangnan.

5. Tradition and Ghosts

In traditional places,
people are many and
ghosts are many, though
one could say people
are few and ghosts
are many, though
one could say
there are only
ghosts.
Listening to
someone

speak, I know
he's a ghost
but have no
wish to bluntly
point it out:
scared of
frightening the
ghost himself
and all
the others
listening.

6.   Dialogue on the Atomic Bomb
A colleague says:
I oppose the
atomic bomb
exploding on
me alone!

Another says:
if one falls
unexploded, it
could just
fall on you!

And another says:
What's your state?
If the bomb
attacks, you run
first. I'll hold it!

7.   Old Actor
Old actor
plays someone
else.
His whole life,
lives sixty lives.

Enough!

Come to the
end of
play-acting,
he savors
everything.

Finally, he gets to play his own death.

Please be quiet. Please turn off the light.

8. Young Actor
All made up and
ready for the
stage, she wears
pink pants and a
pink shirt, her
shoulders bare.

Neither happy nor sad,
like any other little
girl, a moment
before stepping onto
the ancient stage, into
the open air,
she tugs her pants.

—*translated by* 弗莱德 莫顿译 *Fred Moten*

Biographies

Rae Armantrout 雷伊 艾尔曼特罗特

Rae Armantrout's most recent full-length book, *Partly: New and Selected Poems*, was published by Wesleyan University Press in 2016. A chapbook of poems in conversation with physics, *Entanglements*, is forthcoming in February 2017, also from Wesleyan. And *Itself* was published by Wesleyan in 2015. A vinyl record of her reading her poems has just appeared from Fonograf Records/Octopus Books called *Conflation*. Her work has been published in two Spanish language editions in the last year: *Rae Armantrout: Poemas*: Universitat de Valencia (Spain) translated by Natalia Carbajosa and *Recurrencias:* Ediciones sin Nombre (Mexico, 2013). *Just Saying* was published by Wesleyan in 2013. *Versed* (Wesleyan, 2009) received the Pulitzer Prize and the National Book Critics Circle Award. It was also a finalist for the National Book Award. *Next Life* (Wesleyan, 2007) was chosen as one of the 100 Notable Books of 2007 by *The New York Times*. Other recent books include *Money Shot* (Wesleyan, 2011), *Collected Prose* (Singing Horse, 2007), *Up to Speed* (Wesleyan, 2004), *The Pretext* (Green Integer, 2001), and *Veil: New and Selected Poems* (Wesleyan University Press, 2001). Her poems have been included in anthologies such as *short: an international anthology of five centuries of short-short stories, prose poems, brief essays and other short prose forms (Persea, 2014), Privacy Policy: an anthology of Surveillance Poetics* (Black Ocean, 2014), *The Best American Poetry of 2014* (Scribner, 2014), *The Best of the Best American Poetry: 1988-2012* (2013)*, The Norton Anthology of Postmodern American Poetry* (2013), *The Open Door: 100 Poems, 100 Years of Poetry Magazine,* (Chicago, 2012), *American Hybrid* (Norton, 2009), *American Women Poets in the 21st Century: Where Language Meets the Lyric Tradition*, (Wesleyan, 2002), *The Oxford Book of American Poetry* (Oxford, 2006) and *The Best American Poetry* of 1988, 2001, 2002, 2004, 2007, 2008, 2011 and 2012. Armantrout received an award in poetry from the Foundation for Contemporary Arts in 2007 and a Guggenheim Fellowship in 2008. Armantrout was born in Vallejo, California in 1947. She is Professor Emeritus of Poetry and Poetics at the University of California, San Diego.

Mei-mei Berssenbrugge 白萱华

Mei-mei Berssenbrugge is the author of 12 books of poetry, including *Four Year Old Girl* (Kelsey Street Press, 1998), *Empathy* (Station Hill Press, 1999), *I Love Artists: New and Selected Poems* (University of California Press, 2006), and *Hello, the Roses* (New Directions, 2013). She has received a 1976 National Endowment for the Arts Fellowship, a 1980 American Book Award for *Random Possession*, a 1981 National Endowment for the Arts Fellowship, a 1984 American Book Award for *The Heat Bird*, a 1990 National Endowment for the Arts Award, a 1990 PEN West Award for *Empathy*, a 1998 Asian American Literary Award for *Endocrinology*, a 1999 Western States Book Award for *Four Year Old Girl*, and a 2004 Asian American Literary Award for *Nest*. She has collaborated with many artists, including Kiki Smith and her husband, Richard Tuttle. She has collaborated with artists in the book arts and in theatre, including Frank Chin and Tan Dun. *Slow Time*, poems translated into Chinese, was published by Intellectual Property Publishing House in 2016. Berssenbrugge was born in 1947 in Beijing to Chinese and Dutch-American parents, but grew up in the suburbs of Boston, Massachusetts. She lives in northern New Mexico and New York City.

Brandon Brown 布兰登 布朗

Brandon Brown is from Kansas City, Missouri and has lived in the Bay Area since 1998. He is the author of five books of poetry, most recently *The Good Life* (Big Lucks) and *Top 40* (Roof.) He is also the author of several chapbooks, and two collaborative volumes of Christmas poems with J. Gordon Faylor, most recently *A Christmas Reckoning.* Poems and prose have recently appeared in *Art in America, Open Space, Fanzine, Art Practical, New American Writing, The Poetry Project Newsletter,* and *Best American Experimental Writing.* Brown has an MFA from San Francisco State University, where he studied with Stacy Doris, and in 2015 won a fellowship from the National Endowment for the Arts. He is an editor at Krupskaya and occasionally publishes small press materials under the imprint OMG! He lives under the long shadow of little Albany Hill in El Cerrito, California.

Che Qianzi 车前子

Che Qianzi (the pen name of Gu Pan) was born in 1963 in Suzhuo and currently splits his time between his hometown and Beijing. A well-known poet, prose stylist, and painter, Che has published over 30 volumes of poetry, essays and picture albums. Che Qianzi is known as China's "poet's poet." His poetry reflects an experimental disposition. While he is often associated with the Language School of avant-garde American poetry because of his attention to the materiality of language itself, to him, the self in art is just an art, nothing more.

Nada Gordon 娜达 高登

Nada Gordon was born in 1964, in Oakland, California. A prodigy, she began writing poetry at 7, skipped high school, became involved with punk culture as a young teen, and graduated with a BA in Creative Writing in 1984 from San Francisco State University. SFSU overlapped significantly with the vibrant literary community of the Bay Area, which included the L=A=N=G=U=A=G=E Writing group and the New Narrativists. While in the SFSU program she won first place in the Academy of American Poets Student Award, judged by Stephen Rodefer. She attended UC Berkeley for her Master's degree in English Literature and wrote a thesis on the then (and still) largely unexplored works of Bernadette Mayer. While in school she published *more hungry* (voces puerulae, 1985), *rodomontade* (e.g. press, 1985), and *lip* (voces puerulae, 1988). In 1988, she moved to Japan to teach English as a Foreign Language at Kanda Institute of Foreign Languages, Mejiro University, and Chuo University. While in Japan, she assisted with the translation of the tanka of Terayama Shuji, edited a literary magazine, *Aya*, and wrote English language learning textbooks. She returned to the US in 1999 and published several books in short succession: *dolor core recede sanpo* (voces puerulae, 2000), *anime* (voces puerulae, 2000), *foriegnn bodie* (Detour, 2001) based on her time in Japan, *Are Not Our Lowing Heifers Sleeker than Night-Swollen Mushrooms?* (Spuyten Duyvil, 2001), and *Swoon* (Granary Books, 2001) a e-pistolary techno-romantic nonfiction novel. She served for a year as editor of the *Poetry Project Newsletter* and was a curator of the Segue Reading Series for eleven years. She was a founding member of the Flarf Collective. During this period, she published V. *Imp*. (Faux Press, 2003), *Folly* (Roof, 2007), *Scented Rushes* (Roof, 2010), and *Vile Lilt* (Roof, 2013). In her readings, Gordon incorporates song, dance, comedy, costume, video, and other performative aspects, and has performed not only in traditional poetry venues but also at The Whitney Museum and The Museum of Modern Art in New York, The Redcat Theater in Los Angeles, and The

Walker Arts Center in Minneapolis. Her video *The Garden of Life* was featured in the Festival of (In)Appropriation in 2009. She has taught poetry writing workshops at Saint Mark's Poetry Project. In 2012, she traveled to Myanmar to meet Pemskool, a group of young flarf-influenced poets, and gave a presentation on contemporary poetry tendencies in the USA. In 2014, she won the first Stacy Doris Memorial Poetry Award for her poem, "A Thing." Gordon's work has been translated into several languages including Japanese, Dutch, Hebrew, Icelandic, and Burmese. She lives in Brooklyn and coordinates the ESL program at Pratt Institute.

Huang Fan 黄梵

Huang Fan is an associate professor at Nanjing University of Science and Technology. He is the author of three poetry books: *Elegies of Nanjng*, *Taiwan Sings* and *Huang Fan: Selected Poems of a Decade*; three novels: *Until Youth Disappears, The Eleventh Commandment* and *The Floating Colors*, as well as one collection of short stories, *Girl's School Teacher*. Huang Fan also published a collection of essays in 2016, *The Chinese Wanderer*. His works have been awarded the Writers' Golden Prize for Short Story, the Beijing Literary Prize for Poetry, Fangcao Chinese Poetry Prize, the Jinling Literary Prize, The Day After Tomorrow Art and Culture Prize, and fellowships from Cross-Strait Writers' Exchange, Gottingen University and the Henry Luce Foundation. Huang Fan also works as the editor-in-Chief of *Nanjing Review* and *Yangtze River Poetry Journal*. His writings have been translated into German, Italian, Greek, Korean, French, Japanese and English.

Lan Lan 蓝蓝

Lan Lan was born in 1967. Publishing since the age of fourteen, she is considered an influential lyrical poet in contemporary China. Author of nine poetry titles including *Life with a Smile* (1990); *Songs of Romance* (1993); *Inner Life* (1997); *Sleep, Sleep* (2003); and *From Here, to Here* (2008); she also has published three volumes of prose and several collections of children's fiction. Her writings have been translated into English, French, Russian, Spanish, German, Japanese, Korean, Dutch, Belgian and Romanian. Since 2003, she has been invited to many international poetry festivals. Awarded the prestigious Liu Li'an Poetry Prize in 1996, she was voted by a panel of seventy Chinese critics and poets as the top writer of the Best Ten Female Poets. In 2009, she also garnered four of the nation's most important literary awards: The Poetry & People Award (considered the most influential Chinese popular international award), the Yulong Poetry Prize, the Best Ten Poets in China Award and the Bing Xin Children's Literature New Work Award. She lives in Beijing.

Fred Moten 弗雷德 莫顿

Fred Moten was born in 1962 in Las Vegas, Nevada. He teaches and conducts research in black studies, performance studies, poetics and critical theory. He is author of *consent not to be a single being, In the Break: The Aesthetics of the Black Radical Tradition, Hughson's Tavern, B. Jenkins, The Feel Trio, The Little Edges, The Service Porch* and co-author, with Stefano Harney, of *The Undercommons: Fugitive Planning and Black Study* and *A Poetics of the Undercommons*, and, with Wu Tsang, of *Who touched me?* Moten lives in New York and works at New York University.

Na Ye 娜夜

Ms. Na Ye was born in Liaoning Province of Manchurian descent, but grew up in China's northwest region. She graduated from the Chinese Department of Nanjing University. She has published many poetry collections—*Savoring Love, My Cold Lips, Personal Resume,* and *Poems by Na Ye*, etc. She has received a number of accolades including the prestigious Lu Xun Literary Award, The People's Literature Award and The Asking the Heaven Award. She was named one of the Best Ten Young Women poets in the New Millennium. Her works have been translated into English, French, Russian, Japanese and Swedish, etc. Now she lives in Chong Qing, China.

Bob Perelman 鲍勃 帕里

Bob Perelman was one of the early exponents of Language Writing in the Bay Area, an influential strategy of writing that undercut the "norms of persona-centered, 'expressive' poetry." He started *Hills* magazine in 1973 and organized the seminal Talk Series in San Francisco. His books include *Iflife* (Roof Books. 2007), *Ten to One—Selected Poems* (Wesleyan University Press, 1999), *The Future of Memory* (Roof Books, 1998), *Virtual Reality* (Roof Books, 1993), *Face Value* (Roof Books, 1988), *The First World* (Figures, 1986), *To the Reader* (Tuumba Press, 1984), *Primer* (This Press, 1981), *a.k.a.* (Tuumba Press, 1979), *7 Works* (The Figures, 1978), *Braille* (Ithaca House Press. 1975). His poems have been widely anthologized, appearing numerous times in *Best American Poetry* series and in *The Best of the Best American Poetry*. His critical works include *The Trouble with Genius: Reading Pound, Joyce, Stein, and Zukofsky* (University of California Press, 1994), *The Marginalization of Poetry: Language Writing and Literary History* (Princeton University Press, 1996), and *Modernism the Morning After* (Alabama University Press, forthcoming in 2017). He was born in Youngstown, Ohio in 1947. He is Professor Emeritus of English at the University of Pennsylvania.

Wang Xiaoni 王小妮

Born in Chang Chun, China in 1955, Wang Xiaoni spent seven years farming in the countryside during the Cultural Revolution. In 1982, Xiaoni graduated from Jilin University and then worked as an editor at Chang Chun Film Studio. In 1985, she settled in Shenzen and became a professor at Hainan University. She has published over 25 books of poetry including *My Selected Poems* (1986), *On Visiting Friends* (1992-1993), *Exile in Shenzhen* (1994), *My Paper Wraps My Fire* (1997), *Something Crosses My Mind* (2014) among others as well as many essays, short stories and novels. Wang has received numerous awards, including the second annual Chinese Literature Media Award in 2004. In 2015, the translation of her book *Something Crosses My Mind* by Eleanor Goodman was shortlisted for the International Griffin Poetry Prize.

Xi Chuan 西川

Xi Chuan is one of the most influential poets in contemporary China. He is now one of two editors-in-chief of the magazine *Dangdai Gouji Shitan* (*Contemporary World Poetry*). He has published five collections of poems to date. His series of poems (*Flowers in the Mirror* and the *Moon on the Water*) was adapted into an experimental play directed by Meng Jinghui and was presented at the 35th Festival Internacional Cervantino, Mexico, 2007. In 2005, the Italian visual Artist Marco Mereo Rotelli made a giant installation named *Poetry Island* with 12 poems from 12 poets (including Adonis, Yves Bonnefoy, Charles Tomlinson, Tadeusz Rozewicz and Xi Chuan) and exhibited it at the 51st La Biennale di Venezia. The composer Guo Wenjing turned Xi Chuan's poem 'Yuanyou' (Long Journey) into a piece of music and was performed in 2004 by the Hong Kong Philharmonic Orchestra conducted by Edo de Waart.

James Sherry 詹姆斯 谢里

James Sherry is the author of 13 books of poetry and criticism and one of the leading proponents of Language Writing. His books include *The Oligarch: rewriting Machiavelli's* The Prince *for Our Time* (Palgrave, 2017), *Entangled Bank* (Chax, 2016), *Oops! Environmental Poetics* (BlazeVox, 2013), *Four For* (Meow Press, 1995), *Doscapade* (Hot Bird, 1991), *Our Nuclear Heritage* (Sun & Moon Press, 1991), *The Word I Like White Paint Considered* (Awede Press, 1986), *Lazy Sonnets* (Potes and Poets Press, 1986), *Popular Fiction* (ROOF Books, 1985), *Converses* (Awede Press, 1983), *Integers* (DTW, 1980), *In Case* (Sun & Moon Press, 1980), *Part Songs* (Awede Press, 1978). His work has been translated into 8 languages including the Chinese edition of *Selected Language Poems* (Sichuan Literature and Art Publishing House, Chengdu, 1003), translated by Ziqing Zhang and Yunte Huang. He is the editor of Roof Magazine and Roof Books, a seminal poetry publisher, associated with virtually every innovative strategy in English language writing of the past 40 years. He started the Segue Foundation in 1977. Sherry was born in 1946 and lives in New York City.

Sun Dong 孙冬

Sun Dong is a professor at Nanjing University of Finance and Economics, China. Poet and literary critic, she graduated from Nanjing University with Ph.D. in English Literature in 2009. She was a post-doc fellow at McMaster University in Hamilton, Ontario, in 2010. She has published one academic monograph, one poetry book, *The Cruel Crow* (co-authored with Feng Dong), and over a hundred poems in periodicals in China, Canada, America, Romania, Turkey and India.

Poet Translator Matrix

直译 Literal Translations English to Chinese:

Feng Chen/Margaret Ross: Rae Armantrout, Fred Moten, Brandon Brown
Sun Dong/Liuyu Chen/Xiao-bo Yuan: Mei-mei Berssenbrugge, Nada Gordon,
    Bob Perelman

直译 Literal Translations Chinese to English:

Margaret Ross/Feng Chen: Huang Fan, Lan Lan, Na Ye
Xiao-bo Yuan/Sun Dong/Liuyu Chen: Xi Chuan, Che Qianzi
Sun Dong: Wang Xiaoni, final edits of all literals

Chinese poets translated as follows:
Che Qianzi: Fred Moten, Bob Perelman, Mei-mei Berssenbrugge
Huang Fan: Fred Moten, Brandon Brown, Rae Armantrout
Lan Lan: Mei-mei Berssenbrugge, Nada Gordon, Bob Perelman
Na Ye: Rae Armantrout, Nada Gordon, Brandon Brown
Wang Xiaoni: Rae Armantrout, Brandon Brown, Bob Perelman
Xi Chuan: Mei-mei Berssenbrugge, Nada Gordon, Fred Moten

US poets translated as follows:
Rae Armantrout: Wang Xiaoni, Huang Fan, Na Ye
Mei-mei Berssenbrugge: Xi Chuan, Che Qianzi, Lan Lan
Brandon Brown: Wang Xiaoni, Huang Fan, Na Ye
Nada Gordon: Xi Chuan, Lan Lan, Na Ye
Fred Moten: Xi Chuan, Che Qianzi, Huang Fan
Bob Perelman: Wang Xiaoni, Che Qianzi, Lan Lan